Instant
E-Commerce!

Instant E-Commerce!

Kate J. Chase

SYBEX®

San Francisco ◆ Paris ◆ Düsseldorf ◆ Soest ◆ London

Associate Publisher: Cheryl Applewood

Contracts and Licensing Manager: Kristine O'Callaghan

Acquisitions and Developmental Editor: Bonnie Bills

Editor: Donna Crossman

Production Editor: Jennifer Campbell

Technical Editor: Everard Strong

Book Designer: Maureen Forys, Happenstance Type-O-Rama

Electronic Publishing Specialist: Maureen Forys, Happenstance Type-O-Rama

Proofreaders: Leslie E. H. Light, Nancy Riddiough

Indexer: Ted Laux

Cover Design: Gorska Design

Cover Illustration: Caryl Gorska, Gorska Design

This book is dedicated to Robert Pratt and in memory of Arnold Brackman, two very special teachers who helped me hone my craft.

Acknowledgments

Almost no book is the single effort of one person, the author.

Instead, a collection of gifted, wise people come together as part of the process. They help the author shape the focus and content, answer important questions, make certain the work stays on schedule and meets—and hopefully exceeds—the requirements, as the process winds through production and then out to stores.

It is my great pleasure to acknowledge all those who worked with me in the development of this work.

Bonnie Bills, Acquisitions and Developmental Editor, whose very competent, always helpful, and cheerful demeanor made this book a reality—and a better book—from start to finish.

Sean Parsons and George Kearns of Go Daddy Software, who made themselves available for many questions.

The editorial and production team at Sybex—Jennifer Campbell, Donna Crossman, Everard Strong, and Maureen Forys.

Dan Schiff, Archivist, who provided wonderful, much needed help with the creation of the screen shots used in this work.

Neil J. Salkind and the folks at Studio B Literary Agency, who help me find and meet new challenges.

Bill Ball, Tracy Martin, Rick McMillion, CK Phalon, Robert Proffitt, Terri Stratton (with Jack Imsdahl, Al Kuntzler, Deepak Midha, Jane Roberts, and Frank Sugino), and other members of the technical online community where I work and essentially live for their support, their handholding, and their tireless commitment to technical excellence.

John (Chris) Bedell, my partner, who helped both with review and by supplying the author with much needed doses of coffee, Chinese take-out, and salads.

Contents

Contents

Contents

Introduction

Congratulations! Buying this book indicates that you have decided—or at least decided to consider the possibility of deciding—to put the effort into establishing your own Web site on the Internet, probably to promote your shop or business and perhaps conduct sales. For this, you have millions of predecessors, and hundreds of thousands will join you this year.

What are the benefits for establishing an online Web presence for your business or store? The biggest benefit is that it has the potential for providing you with increased sales by opening your store shelves to a more global shopping audience who may otherwise never make it to your business or store. If establishing your Web presence has always sounded like a daunting endeavor, you'll see, by using this book and the WebSite Complete software, how quick, easy, and inexpensively this can be done.

How This Book Is Organized

The Contents and Index sections will help you move through this book and are useful especially if you're like me and not always a linear reader. The 11 chapters and appendix have been laid out in the way that I think you'd be most apt to progress through the material: moving from a basic understanding of the World Wide Web and the included software, WebSite Complete v4.0, and then forward through planning and implementing your e-commerce site.

Chapter 1, "Internet, Web Site, and E-Commerce Basics," explains the brief history of online small business commerce and the Web itself. It also covers how most people connect to the Internet, how their connection affects how fast they'll be able to access your Web, and how that, in turn, affects how you design it. It also discusses some of the intricacies of Web site development that you're saved from doing by using a comprehensive one-package Web site solution like WebSite Complete.

Chapter 2, "Getting Started with WebSite Complete 4.0," takes you through installing the software and preparing it to help you set up your site.

Chapter 3, "Planning Your First E-Commerce Site," helps you understand the basic collection of pages that will make up your Web site, and then takes you beyond to thinking about the extra pages or features and overall atmosphere you want to develop.

Chapter 4, "Building Your First E-Commerce Web Site," explains how the software Desktop is set up for your use, and walks you through the steps necessary to modify the overall look of your site and add or modify text and images. These steps result in completion of a basic, commercially oriented Web site.

Chapter 5, "Adding Special Features to your E-Commerce Web Site," explains the plug-ins and other extras you can add to your site to give it either extra functionality (like calculators and property listings for real estate sites) or pizzazz (like fancy scrolling marquees and Flash animations for dramatic entry screens).

Chapter 6, "Publishing Your E-Commerce Web Site," explains the final steps necessary to check your site for problems before you post it to your Web hosting service. It then explains how to publish your site to the Internet.

Chapter 7, "Revising Your Published E-Commerce Site," identifies how to test your site once it's published to identify issues you want to change, how to make those changes, and how to republish your site.

Chapter 8, "Diagnosing and Curing Common Web Site Problems," describes some of the most frequently seen issues with new Web sites and how to resolve them.

Chapter 9, "Building Your Online Store," explains how you can create an online store with WebSite Complete. It also details what a merchant account is and how to apply for one so that you can let shoppers pay by credit card and have those charges promptly paid to your account.

Chapter 10, "Promoting Your E-Commerce Web Site," discusses how you can use basic communications means—business cards, flyers, your Web site address added to advertisements—as well as online Web search engines to attract visitors to your Web site.

Chapter 11, "Maintaining and Managing Your E-Commerce Web Site," describes common issues seen in sites that are not frequently updated and checked and how you can avoid them.

The Appendix, "Help with Using WebSite Complete," discusses how to resolve various issues such as developing, publishing, and managing your site with the software.

Conventions Used in This Book

I used several conventions in this book to highlight important or interesting material.

For example, when you see words in this **font**, it tells you to look in the margin for a definition. You will find several **margin definitions** as you read through this book, and you can also find these listed again in the glossary.

margin definition
in the margins you'll find definitions of e-commerce terms

Note

Read these Notes for additional information you should know as you proceed.

Tip

When you see a Tip like this one, check it out for extra help or timesaving tips you should find very useful in developing your site and working with WebSite Complete.

Warning

Pay special attention when a Warning appears because it will advise you of problems you may encounter if you either don't follow the steps or make an unusual selection.

As you read, be aware that you'll find special formatting for information that needs your special attention. For example, `program font` is used for `code`, `URLs`, `filenames`, and `paths`. Also, anything you will need to type is in bold **font**. (Sometimes there's a combination of the two.)

A Few Words from the Author

When I first started using the World Wide Web (WWW)—back when it was first implemented in the early 1990s—I was both dazzled and confused. The dazzle was because the Web and the browser I viewed it with had nice colors and pictures and understandable text. The confusion came from wondering, "OK, how do they do this? How did they make this Web page? How did they get that icon to rotate?" I'll tell you how I handled this curiosity in a minute.

The Internet as we used to know it was usually accessed from clunky programs with interfaces that were far from intuitive. Often, you had to already know a little bit of the kind of language old-time Internet administrators used in order to find or do *anything*.

After all, before the Web, you usually found nice-looking graphics—and tools for helping you navigate around to different areas and online help—only if you subscribed to an online service such as CompuServe, Prodigy, or America Online. For this extra assistance and color, you paid a lot more money than these services typically charge today. And in those days, the online services weren't the Internet companies they are today: They operated as private services that subscribers could connect to and that locked out nonsubscribers—leading some to call them cyber country clubs. These services didn't have gateways or any other ways to access the Internet until after the Internet became better known and desired by customers.

Early online stores were largely based on these online services. The offerings tended to be few because most people had very slow modems, and slower modems meant that every time users wanted to look at a new item or in a new area, they had to wait for the bits and bytes to go back and forth between their PC and the network they dialed into. It had all the fun of watching paint dry. The high hourly connection rates meant online users might not want to linger at any one store because a long shopping trip, whether a purchase was made or not, could get expensive. Shoppers didn't always spend time browsing. Instead, they looked for a particular item, then got out fast. Also, the online audience was much smaller than the almost 50 percent of U.S. households who access the Web today.

With these online services, online ordering was nearly nonexistent. When you could find what you wanted, you were more than likely directed to a phone number, or you gave your confidential credit card number in unsecured e-mail to place an order. So a business or commercial Web site served as more of a large business card than a true online store.

Another disadvantage for business owners under the old system was that only big-name sellers had the opportunity to set up shop in a storefront on one of these online services. As the online world began to attract the interest of the average consumer (and each service battled to have the most subscribers among these newly wired people), online services preferred to give space to those products that would help them capture a much bigger audience. K-Mart, Lands' End, and Sears were considered worthy, while many smaller companies, let alone one- or two-person shops, were not. A family-owned business that produced a limited number of custom-made products each week—say, a Vermont-based leather slipper company that hand-sews 50 pairs each week—just didn't have much of a chance at getting online to capture a market or just make some sales.

This paralleled the phenomenon that small downtown businesses had seen in the late 1970s through the 1990s, when the strong influence of malls and super centers caused downtown shopping in many communities to dry up and go out of business. Stores that had neither the inventory nor the financial resources to move into these malls were losing customers to the glitzy new places that offered a host of different stores all within one space.

However, that trend is changing at the beginning of the new century. Because of high rents, malls in many communities are struggling to keep a full complement of stores, and they're seeing fewer shoppers. But where are the shoppers going? According to some national organizations devoted to trying to repopulate downtown business and shopping areas, customers are not just going back into local areas to shop, they're going online. So what are the small downtown businesses and shops doing? They're going online to recapture some of the market they lost years ago to the malls. And there's more. These smaller, local vendors are grabbing shoppers beyond their geographic region and reaching a more global marketplace.

Let me share an example: I recently moved from Connecticut to very rural Vermont. One of my biggest concerns with the move was how I would find the goods and services I needed now that I was so far removed from even so much as a bustling downtown area, let alone shopping centers and malls. Even on some large state roads up here, you can go quite a distance without being able to find so much as a cup of coffee.

Finally, I began to find my way around up here as I slowly discovered small grocery stores and bookshops, hardware shops, and little places to eat. But as I discovered them, I discovered something else—a lot of them have set up shop on the Web. An Internet address printed on the price tag of my meat reminds me to log on to check for weekly specials. Another Internet address appearing on the marker of the books I buy tells me I can check out the bookstore's most recent arrivals on their Web site, which is likely to get me into the store again to find things they haven't advertised on their site. A label on a coffee cup I bought from a local pottery studio brought me to a Web site where I ordered some holiday gifts from other vendors paired with the studio.

None of these businesses are very large. Almost all of them are owner-operated, and the owner runs the physical business and easily manages the business Web site around slower times in the regular work. And all of them are taking advantage of the low initial cost and operation of setting up a Web site that both enhances services for their current customers and opens the door to a new audience. This is an audience who may never happen onto the street in the town or city where the business is located but who can order a product quickly and securely over the Internet.

So how did I satisfy my curiosity about how Web designers create the things you see on a good Web site? I spent time learning how they did it by devouring books and online help sites devoted to HTML and Web design techniques and watching what worked and what didn't. That study certainly took a lot more time than I would have liked. Then, after I mastered the basics and moved to a comfortable level of skill, I realized that the things I wanted most to achieve—the ability to plug into a Web site certain functionalities that are created in more advanced programming and scripting languages—were already available in packages I could buy off the shelf and customize for my needs.

This book and the accompanying software are designed to move you rapidly from Web novice to a published e-commerce site designer and manager without all the confusion, mystery, expense, and work I experienced when I first started.

−Kate Chase, rural Vermont

Chapter 1

Internet, Web Site, and E-Commerce Basics

Tens of thousands of new Web sites will go online this year. Of those, up to 50 percent may be specifically created to promote a business or commercial enterprise, and, in turn, a percentage of those will have a unique advantage for entrepreneurs: the ability to sell products and services via the Internet. But because of the daunting recent economic news about the precarious nature of Internet sales, perhaps we should take a moment to consider what is happening in these choppy waters before we jump in.

E-Commerce Today

e-commerce

the practice of selling products and services directly from an online location, such as a Web site or an online service

The term **e-commerce**, or electronic commerce, gets tossed around both online and on the evening news. E-commerce basically refers to the buying and selling of products and services electronically. This can be done through a Web site, which presents goods and services to potentially anyone around the globe via the Internet, or through a site within a larger service with a specific target audience. An example of the latter is an online store on America Online© that only AOL members can reach.

Some very large companies have tossed tens of millions of dollars into developing a large Internet presence through splashy, innovative Web sites complete with every bell and whistle. Many of them had such a high initial or subsequent expenditure that they are still struggling a few years later to see any kind of profit from their effort, and some have gone out of business.

For example, Dell Computers, one of the largest and most successful business and consumer PC manufacturers, estimates that U.S. companies and businesses will spend approximately $200 billion on their Internet sites/infrastructures in the year 2002, while Jupiter Communications estimates about $41 billion in revenue from e-commerce the same year. Most of us could not run either our homes or small businesses with this kind of economic divide.

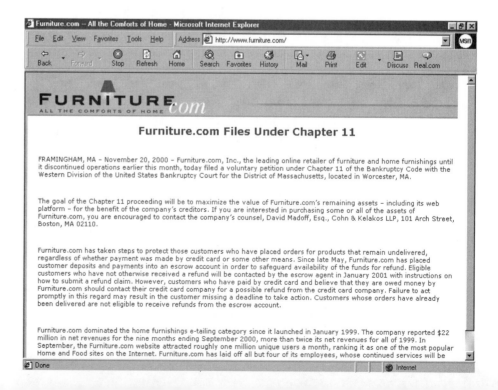

By the beginning of the year 2001, we've seen the failure of some notable companies that were once considered very hot Internet properties, including furniture.com, garden.com, pets.com, eToys.com, and valueamerica.com. After garnering a lot of attention when they debuted and then becoming household names—at least among the Internet consumer crowd—they disappeared from the net landscape without much notice. Others, such as the large bookseller amazon.com, have had to wrestle to stay atop the ever-rising heap.

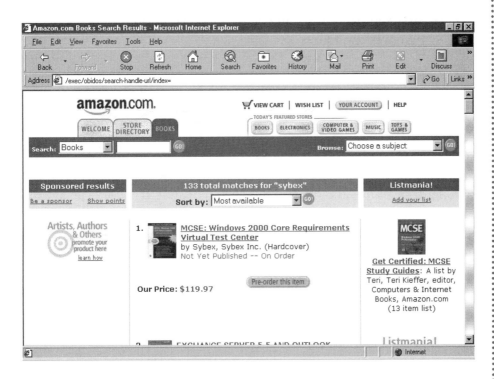

These are, however, firms with high overhead. The cost of early success is often a need to spend loads of money to expand quickly; if the initial success is fleeting, a company can wind up showing a lot more red in its accounts than black. The larger the company, the more revenue it needs to keep going.

On the other hand, a smaller company, particularly a business run (mostly) by one or two key people, doesn't have quite the same concerns and normally won't be subject to as much risk. A large company anticipating millions in sales each year might have to buy a great deal of new equipment to handle the Web operation; hire a staff of Web professionals, online sales specialists, and people to handle order processing and shipping; and pay large sums for heavy volume Internet speed and capacity.

Web host provider

an individual or company that provides space to host a Web site, making it available to the public via the Internet and a Web browser

A small operation doesn't need that much to create and produce a Web site capable of handling online transactions. What is required is a desire to accomplish the goal, some space on a hard drive to create the files for the Web site, the basic files needed to establish that site along with the knowledge of how to create them, and an account with a **Web host provider**.

 Note

An account with a Web host provider can cost anywhere from $9.95 a month on up, depending on the features and services needed.

One of those requirements can be fulfilled much more easily through the use of a package such as WebSite Complete, published by Go Daddy Software. Most of us probably have better things to do with our time than to learn the intricacies of formatting a Web page for a site. WebSite Complete, therefore, has the knowledge to take care of a lot of the creation. Even if the goal is to put together a fairly simple e-commerce site to start, using this program can still save weeks, if not months, of development time.

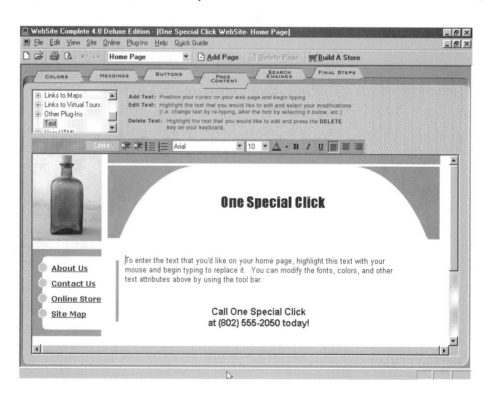

Anatomy of a Web Site

Most Web sites aren't just one static page, as is a printed page of text. A site is usually a combination of pages written in a basic language—HTML (Hypertext Markup Language)—that makes them viewable by a Web browser. These pages are bound together by a common purpose or theme (sports, news, products offered by a company, services offered by a group) and linked together either by **hypertext links** or through **navigational buttons**, both of which help a visitor move through a site's pages. If the pages include images to display, such as a business logo or a product photo, the images must be provided in a format recognizable by Web browsers and included as separate files. The details of how Web sites are organized and how they work will be discussed later in this chapter.

How E-Commerce Sites Are Different

The process of producing a personal Web site is relatively simple once the user learns how to place pictures on a page and work the text around them. Ceating a Web site with the intent of selling some business or service is much more complex, and the amount of complexity depends on what's being offered. Some Web sites are used like online billboards, referring visitors to a phone number, e-mail, or even a physical store or office location to conduct actual business. Such sites require a good design technique, but not a lot of extra finesse, and are not e-commerce sites because nothing is "sold" online.

E-commerce sites need to incorporate many components, from simple text to the ability to process financial transactions. For example, an e-commerce site can offer some basic information about its business that will encourage visitors to feel they can buy something from it. The site should have compelling content in the form of articles and clear, well-written product/service descriptions to encourage visitors to shop there. Also, potential customers need to have a way to reach the business if they have a problem using the Web site. Sites selling goods need to plug in a way to actually perform transactions on the Web site, usually by means of the customer's credit card information, which then needs

hypertext link (hyperlink)
special text on a Web page that, when clicked upon, opens a related page on the same or different Web site

navigational buttons
buttons used on a Web site, with labels such as Back and Next, that, when clicked upon, help a visitor move through the various pages of the site (or a long list of products and services available, such as in an online catalog)

to be processed so that the business gets its money and the customer gets the order. (The latter may not be necessary for selling services. A site could sell memberships in a service or a whole package of services using the transaction process, for example.)

The flow of a typical online transaction is shown below:

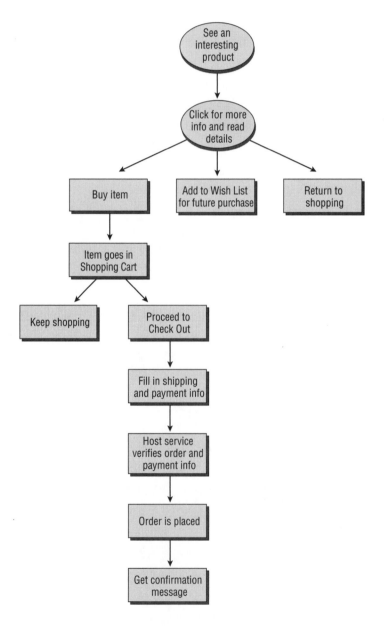

Transaction processing is one area in which a one-step solution software package like WebSite Complete truly comes in handy. Other notable Web page–creation software, such as Microsoft FrontPage, doesn't come equipped to build an online storefront right out of the box. And without that feature, the user either needs to buy a special program that makes it possible to do online transactions and customize it to work with other Web-creation software, or needs to learn some Web-based programming techniques to create the system from scratch. The former can take some serious money, depending on what the customer chooses to buy and use, and the latter can add months of time spent learning how to do the programming—even many computer professionals don't find designing applications that easy to do.

Online Transactions on a Web Site

When developing a site, the function that takes the most time is plugging in the components for online transactions. Here's a bare minimum of what happens on a Web site that has products to sell:

1. The customer is presented with product options, perhaps in a list format or by an array of small images (called thumbnails) of the products with a title beneath each.

2. The customer chooses a product by clicking its image or title.

3. The customer is then presented with a full description of the product, along with a larger, better-quality image of the item.

4. From the product screen, the customer has several possible options, including the following:

   ◇ a link to delivery and shipping information

   ◇ an option to display a list of similar products

   ◇ an option, such as an Additional Info button, to solicit more information from the vendor about the product

   ◇ a Contact Us option for reaching the vendor with general questions or comments about the online site

   ◇ an option, such as a Buy button, that the customer can click to begin the ordering process

5. Should the customer opt to buy, the item must be deposited in the Shopping Cart to either continue shopping or go straight to Check Out.

6. At Check Out, the customer has these available options:

◆ the ability to review and verify that the information is correct about the product they wish to order (right quantity, right item), and make changes as necessary

◆ the option to cancel the order, if desired

◆ a prompt to provide payment information (usually a credit card), including the Billing and Ship To addresses

 Note

Behind the scenes, this also means the ability of the host site to process that payment (for example, run the credit card number and obtain an authorization code).

◆ a final prompt to submit the order for placement

Tip

Don't undertake this process without first getting a real feel for how online stores do business. Look at both large and small online sales sites and take notes about what is effective and what should be avoided. Then keep these notes handy when planning a Web site in Chapter 3, "Planning Your First E-Commerce Site." Here are some good general e-commerce sites you can check out: bn.com, buy.com, cdnow.com, crateandbarrel.com, deananddeluca.com, macys.com, outpost.com, and pier1.com.

An e-commerce site also has to be able to assure customers that the information they provide as part of the transaction (address, phone number, credit card information, and so on) is secure, meaning that only the vendor will have access to the private data customers provide. Site security is no small feat, and requires an advanced understanding of how the Internet and the browsers that view it work and how to shield the data from unwanted eyes.

At this stage, it's hard for a beginner to even imagine how to put this all together in a Web site. I definitely couldn't when I started. An e-commerce–enabled Web site presents a challenge even to a Web designer with some experience. To more fully appreciate how much easier an integrated Web-creation solution like Web-Site Complete makes the process, a beginner should understand a little more about how the Internet and its WWW (World Wide Web) work, the elements involved in designing an effective Web site, why and how to publish the site to a special type of server called a Web server, the roles and requirements of operating an e-commerce site, and how to work with the site to keep it fresh and the information valuable. The rest of this chapter will explore these topics in preparation for the work ahead.

The Internet: A Global Pipeline for Information

Although the World Wide Web and the Internet have become synonymous, the Web is actually just one part of a whole entity known as the Internet. The Web is the graphical part of the Net and is accessible using a Web browser such as

Microsoft® Internet Explorer, Netscape©, or Opera, which allows for a relatively easy display of pictures and sound. Other parts of the Internet, including IRC (Internet Relay Chat), FTP (File Transfer Protocol), or special areas for file transfer, electronic mail, and **newsgroups**, tend to be functional and informational—and without frills.

newsgroups
messaging areas devoted to particular topics

The Web is the newest major component of the Internet, getting its start in 1993, while other Internet platforms started more than 20 years before. These early platforms were largely used only by the military and defense industry, as well as colleges and universities, so what was out in cyberspace then was mostly dry, text-only reading. The Web is arguably what drew in so many millions around the globe and is credited, in part, with bringing the Internet to the masses.

Now some people think that the Internet exists as one huge supercomputer that everyone dials into. But it's actually a complex global network of computers and communication routes that tie different areas of a country, as well as other countries, together through a common pipeline of sorts. It's this common pipeline that makes the site that someone creates and publishes from their home or office available to their neighbors, to people many states away, and to people accessing the Internet from China or Saudi Arabia or New Zealand.

Connecting to the Internet

Dialing into the Internet actually means connecting to an ISP (Internet Service Provider). An ISP could be an online service such as America Online, a high-speed cable or DSL (digital subscriber line) provider like Time Warner or Verizon™, or a separate service such as EarthLink™ or AT&T WorldNet®. Once the Internet user connects to their provider, they are sharing the provider's high-speed, high-capacity connection to the Internet. However, many providers also don't have a direct connection to the Internet; they buy their time from another company, which may connect to the Internet through yet another entity. In some ways, it's like the world's largest telephone party line, except that it's bits and bytes, not human voices, singing on these lines.

Because the user shares connect time through the provider (and that provider's provider, and so on), they're competing with everyone else who is also connected. This phenomenon, loosely called net traffic (and traffic on the Internet continues to grow by leaps and bounds), explains why connections may seem much faster during some sessions yet much slower during others—and why the same Web site that opens in a couple of seconds on Tuesday morning may seemingly take forever to load on Friday night.

Connection Speeds

Speed is always a consideration when working with Web sites. Connection speeds affect how fast a Web site can load in a browser, how fast new material publishes to a Web site, and how fast people can access a site. A very slow connection can be more prone to errors, and may leave a potential customer on an e-commerce site unable to bring up a picture of the product they want to buy. Or the customer's browser may experience a connection **time-out** before they can place their order. So then they have to decide whether to try to place the order again, or just leave the site.

time-out
a specified time that the Web server waits to respond before it decides that the server isn't going to respond and it should stop trying

Most people who access the Internet still do so with slow connections over old phone lines, not with today's high-speed connections such as DSL and cable modems. The age of these lines contributes noise and other problems that diminish the ability of a 56K modem to connect anywhere near that speed. This must be taken into account when planning a Web site (see Chapter 3). For example, a big page with lots of graphics and animations (where objects on the screen move or change) may not download properly if connecting via old telephone lines.

Servers and the Web

Whatever the user chooses to do on the Internet—check e-mail, participate in an online chat, upload a file, or visit a Web page—they're being routed from their ISP to the "place" that runs what they want to visit. This place is usually a server, with a particular address (my Web site set up through a commercial Web host, for example, has an Internet address of 208.132.195.53 that can also be reached by typing the address **www.reluctanttech.com** in the Web browser's address window).

Web servers

computers running specialized software that handles the behind-the-scenes publishing of Web sites to the Internet and that processes requests from visitors

traffic

the amount of visitors accessing a particular Web site, often measured in unique users per day, per week, or per month (with a server or online service, it refers to the number of people accessing the system during any given time)

A server is usually a dedicated computer or network device that acts to manage the resources on the network—think of a computer with special software running on it to handle the clients (users, other PCs, etc.) that connect to it. There are many types of servers. Mail servers deliver and send e-mail; chat servers host live online discussions; database servers are dedicated to database access, storage, and retrieval; and **Web servers** stage a Web site for availability on the Internet and try to manage the visitors, or **traffic**, coming to the site.

There are also many types of Web servers. A Web server can be as small and simple as a special program running on a home or office computer that sets up an area on a user's hard disk (similar to setting up folders) as a Web-publishing area. With this type, depending on how the user connects to the Internet—or to other computers on a home or office network—and how they have set up their PC to share files, they may be able to let others visit their local Web site. (For security purposes, this isn't necessarily a good idea. People other than those desired may be able to access the contents of a disk-based Web site or other PC files.)

At the other end of the spectrum are banks of dedicated systems allowing for thousands of simultaneous connections and capable of handling them quickly and efficiently. A major Internet presence like Microsoft or Amazon would need this type of Web server just to manage its operations. But many of these larger Web server setups—known as Web hosts or Web host providers—are actually run by separate companies and their capacity is split into any number of smaller companies and single-proprietor businesses. These smaller businesses, in turn, need the power and performance of a commercial server but can't afford their own. It's like renting virtual office or store space at a fraction of the cost of renting physical workspace, with the added advantage of having the Web host provide any equipment needed beyond the actual Web site contributions.

Note

There will be more about Web host providers later in this chapter, as well as in Chapter 3 and Chapter 6, "Publishing Your E-Commerce Web Site," where site planning and publishing will be discussed.

Establishing a Site: The Basic Steps

So much can go into creating a good Web site that it often takes a very large and detailed book to cover just the essentials. No software package will completely take the work out of your hands, either. Some of the key work involves a human mind to mold the content of the site and human eyes to scan for what looks good and what doesn't.

Note

You'll cover many of these steps in greater detail in subsequent chapters, so don't worry if you feel you don't get something now. Remember, too, that when you begin to use WebSite Complete 4.0 to build your site, you'll find that the package takes care of many of the details for you. However, the evolution of your Web site shouldn't feel like magic—it should be a process you understand. If you know what each step accomplishes and why it's important, you should feel more confident about the work you're doing and the site you're developing, and you'll be better able to tailor your site to your business needs and make adjustments when and where you need to do so.

Here are the seven major steps to getting your Web site up and running and then fine-tuning it:

- Choose to create a Web site.
- Plan what you want the site to include and how to proceed.
- Choose a Web host.
- Create the basic, essential Web page(s) for your site.
- Publish the site to a Web server.
- Test the site to make sure it's all working properly.
- Make changes as necessary, including regular updates.

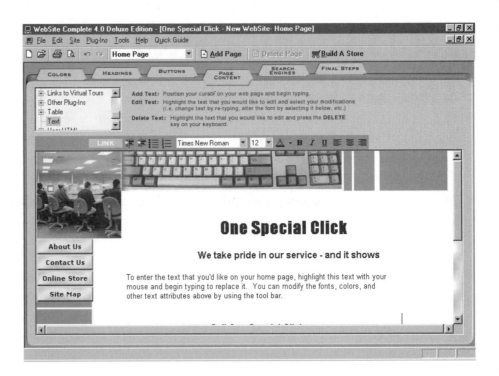

Each of these steps will be covered separately in the following sections.

Choosing to Create a Web Site

This may be a decision you've already made. If so, proceed to the next step. Some of you, however, may still be sitting on the fence between the way you used to do business in a physical location and the way business is done today in cyberspace. Your business may even need to service your customers in both ways.

Creating and setting up a Web site is a very attainable goal, and how involved you make the online portion of your business is up to you. You can set up a site to sell a few specific products as a test of marketability (since you're now selling to customers outside your local area), or you can design one that carries your entire line of products and/or services. In choosing a Web host provider, you can select one that offers the services you specifically need. You also can choose how aggressively you promote your Web site, as you'll read about in depth in Chapter 10, "Promoting Your E-Commerce Web Site."

If you're still uncertain whether you should jump on the Internet sales band-wagon or not, you should be better able to decide how to proceed based on the information in this book. Here are some examples of small businesses that have chosen to use the Internet as at least one—if not the only—means of selling their work or services:

- a small publisher in northern New England who uses his Web site to both promote his titles and allow visitors to order copies online

- an artist and small art gallery owner in Los Angeles who sells both her own work and the work of others by displaying digital pictures of the art online

- an electronics store owner in New Mexico who doubled his sales by offering specialty parts and accessories, as well as his line of audio and video equipment, on his Web site

- an antiques dealer in rural Pennsylvania who went from selling an occasional piece through online auctions (and paying a fee to do so) to selling some of his work on his own Web site

- a craftsperson in Montana who displays examples of his woodworking on his site, and allows customers to place custom orders selected from special features and finishes

- a bed-and-breakfast in Florida that allows customers to make accom-modations online and also sells items from local craftspeople online

- a small family-based moccasin maker in Vermont who takes orders for hand-sewn, custom-made slippers

- a caterer in the Chicago area who not only allows customers to initiate and purchase catering packages online, but also uses her site to sell specialty baked cookies

- a former video store owner in upstate New York who used his site to sell off the inventory of his store, and now sells special-subject videos on his site as a lucrative sideline

There are literally thousands of applications for which an e-commerce site may potentially boost sales and widely expand the range of consumers who will get to see the products being offered.

Planning

This is the most important step in the creation of your Web site, because a good online selling site should be laid out with all the care of a good physical store.

In the planning phase there are a number of choices to be made, including the following:

◆ the focus and overall atmosphere of the site you want to develop

◆ the organization of the site: how it will be laid out and how potential customers will move through the site to find what they want

◆ the products and/or services you want to offer

◆ the methods of payment potential customers can use to make purchases

◆ the nuts-and-bolts considerations, such as which software you'll use to develop the site, how you will make the site available on the Internet (Web hosting), and how much this may cost

During the planning phase, the basic question to ask yourself is whether you want to devote the time to learning how to create a Web site from scratch or use Web-development software to help you do the job. There are some pros and cons to either choice. Learning yourself could ultimately afford you a valuable new set of skills and give you added flexibility in making changes.

The downside to this, however, is that you will need to learn quickly a great deal of technical material (some fairly difficult). While most basic Web sites can be produced using a text editor (like Notepad in Windows), you first have to know the basic formatting language of the World Wide Web: Hypertext Markup Language, or HTML. Then you'll need to develop advanced HTML skills that will make your Web site look professional (as opposed to what a 12-year-old wunderkind could put together).

Here's a snippet of the very start of the HTML source encoding for my Web site. While this snippet sets up some of the initial site information and formatting, I haven't even started getting into the real site content with this:

```
<html>
<head>
<meta http-equiv="Content-Type" content="text/html;
charset=iso-8859-1">
<title>Revised Kate Chase page</title>
```

```
</head>
<body bgcolor="#666633">
<!- BEGIN LINKEXCHANGE CODE ->
<table border="0" cellspacing="0" cellpadding="1"
bgcolor="#0000FF">
 <tr>
  <td>
   <div align="right">
    <table border="0" cellspacing="0" cellpadding="0">
   <tr>
    <td>
     <p align="center"><a
```

Confusing enough? And this is just the start. Most e-commerce Web sites just don't lend themselves well to straight HTML use, because they need to be able to conduct financial transactions. This requires a yet more advanced level of Web understanding, calling into play a knowledge of Web-based programming, such as CGI scripting or **Java**.

Java
the programming language of the Internet

If you're not ready to tackle this—and many aren't—then your planning stage is likely to involve getting a Web package tool like the WebSite Complete 4.0 software.

Choosing a Web Host

A Web host provider lets you rent out some of their space and capacity to publish your site for a fee (usually monthly). Many of the answers to questions you have in the planning process will factor into your choice of Web host.

While word-of-mouth recommendations from friends and associates who have some experience working with Web hosts can help, you should pick your Web host carefully based upon a number of factors. These factors include the following:

- ◆ Does the Web host support the software you'll use to develop your Web site?

- ◆ Does the Web host permit commercial operations (not all do)?

- ◆ Does the Web host directly support secured financial transactions so that your customers can order directly from the Web site?

- ◆ Does the Web host support the use of your own domain name (the identifying name of your Web site, registered through a recognized agency)?

- ◆ Does the Web host provide good support and have a reliable operation (a downed host means a downed site and that can mean lost sales)?

This is an important selection for your potential commercial success, and you should select a Web host before you get too deeply into the creation of your site. If not, and you choose a host that doesn't directly support the type of software you're using or doesn't handle financial transactions as you planned, you may have to change a lot of the work you've already done.

Creating the Essential Site

At this stage, you're ready to use the software you've purchased to help you design the site and then work with it to achieve the results you desire, based on the planning you did in the previous step.

Earlier in this chapter, you learned that most Web sites aren't one static page, but a group of Internet-ready documents linked together, with supporting files such as graphics. In fact, even a small e-commerce site offering a limited range of products can have quite a few pages. Besides these pages and files, the site also needs some sort of organization for how visitors can navigate through it.

Here's a quick glance at the roster of pages (and files) needed to support the Web site of a small book vendor:

- ◆ the home page (often called `default.htm` or `index.htm`), the first page visitors see when they access the Web site, with links to all other main areas of the site

- ◆ the About Us page, a page that talks about the business and those who run it

- ◆ a products page, a major listing of the categories of products available on the site (for example, a book seller might have products grouped into categories like Fiction, Nonfiction, Education, and Children's) with links to separate pages for each of these categories

- ◆ individual product pages, separate pages containing information about and usually a picture of the product, with options that allow the visitor to begin the ordering process

- ✪ payment and shipping pages, which explain payment options and shipping/delivery options

- ✪ ordering pages, where your customers can fill out the information necessary to receive their orders

- ✪ links for moving backward through the site to review product or other information

Here again is where an integrated Web site–development package like WebSite Complete can provide invaluable assistance and reduce the number of details you need to juggle.

Publishing the Site

Once you've finished planning and creating, it's time to publish the site—a slightly fancy term for moving the work you create for your site to its proper final location on the Web host provider's server to make it available to the public.

Very basic sites can get away with using simple upload tools to move the pages to their proper location. Products like WebSite Complete help automate the process for you so that with one or two clicks of your mouse, the files transfer to the Web host and your site is published. Chapter 6 will tell you in detail how to do this.

Testing the Site

One very regrettable error many new Web masters make is thinking their job is done once the essential contents of a site have been published to the Web server. This isn't true in any event—and certainly not true if they're using the site as a professional or business connection. After all, the work should *begin* when they publish the site, as that's when customers will begin to place orders. Each time a page is published for the first time or later modified, the site should be rechecked to be sure everything is as it should be.

In the testing stage, you should always look at the site the way your most difficult customer—or your mother perhaps—might view it, looking for errors, omissions, and imperfections.

Things to look for include the following:

- ◇ Check for spelling and grammar mistakes.
- ◇ Check for overall readability and viewability.
- ◇ Check for problems (including excessive slowness) loading the page.
- ◇ Check that links to other pages on the site (or elsewhere) connect correctly.
- ◇ Make sure that graphics correspond to the text and vice versa.
- ◇ Check each and every product on the site all the way through to order placement. You need to make sure it works for you; if not, it won't work for customers either and you lose sales.

Fine-Tuning the Site

Fine-tuning a Web site should indeed be a constant process. This involves making not only any corrections during the testing process, but also adjustments you feel should be made to enhance the overall atmosphere, information level, or focus of the site.

In addition, sites can become very dated, for a number of reasons:

- ◇ the use of seasonal material that isn't removed once the season has passed
- ◇ an old date of creation or last modification, which tells visitors a Web site isn't being updated regularly
- ◇ the inventory or information never changes, which potentially indicates that either the site isn't being updated or the vendor isn't moving many products
- ◇ links to other sites or other pages on the same site no longer work

Thus, you'll learn more as you move through the book about how to prevent or remedy such situations to keep your site looking fresh, functional, and worthy of someone's shopping dollar.

Chapter 2

Getting Started with WebSite Complete 4.0

You're probably eager to start working with the software and developing your first online, e-commerce–ready site. First things first, however. In this chapter, you'll step through the process of installing WebSite Complete 4.0. You'll also learn what information WebSite Complete will prompt you to provide the first time you run the program. From this chapter, you'll get your first peek at what's possible for your business site using this product just minutes after you begin to install the software.

Preparing for the Software

To begin, you need a copy of WebSite Complete 4.0, some room on your PC's hard drive—65MB minimum if you're using this book's CD-ROM—and a relatively short period of time to install the software and begin using WebSite Complete. Compared to learning HTML to get started, the process is very quick indeed.

Getting WebSite Complete

You'll find your WebSite Complete 4.0 CD packed in the back of this book. Just remove it from its packaging and you're almost ready to start installing.

If you need another copy of the CD or you have friends or colleagues who would like to try it, it can be ordered from Go Daddy by calling (480) 824-1300 or faxing (480) 824-1499. The software can be ordered or downloaded from the manufacturer's Web site at www.godaddy.com.

 Note

It costs $14.95 to download Website Complete. If you order the CD with the Bonus Software and User's Guide, the cost is the same plus $6.50 for shipping and handling.

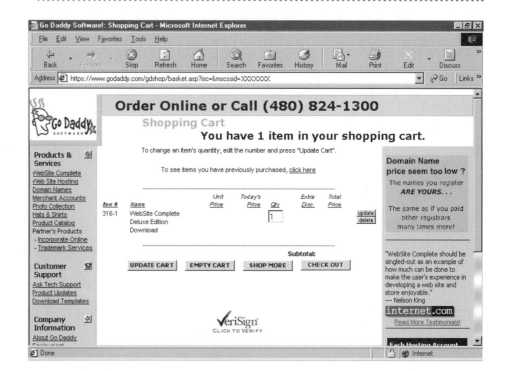

Note

If you misplace your CD and later need to download the software, be aware that there are slight differences between the CD and downloadable versions. The CD not only includes the software and User's Guide, but also has a selection of bonus software you'll read about later in this chapter.

Checking the System Requirements

As with any application, before you attempt to install WebSite Complete 4.0, you should make certain your PC meets the basic system requirements. If your PC doesn't meet this standard, it's possible the application will still install, but it might not work as designed.

System Requirements FAQ

These questions and answers can help you get your system ready for working with WebSite Complete.

Question: Which version of Internet Explorer am I running?

Answer: To check for a current IE installation, go to Start ➤ Programs and look for Internet Explorer. If it's there, double-click it to run the program. In the browser, select the Help menu, choose About, and read the version number supplied there; the first two numbers after Version are the ones to note.

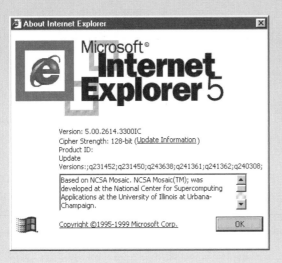

System Requirements FAQ (continued)

Question: It says I have to use Microsoft Internet Explorer 5.0 or later, but I like to use Netscape. What can I do?

Answer: You can continue to use Netscape, or another browser such as Opera, for your regular Web browsing, but Internet Explorer is required by WebSite Complete to help you develop your Web site. Once your site is published, however, it can be accessed using any Web browser you desire.

Question: How much RAM and hard-disk space do I have available?

Answer: For RAM information from Windows 95/98/Me, go to Windows Control Panel, double-click the System icon, and choose the General tab. Your amount of recognized, installed RAM is listed at the bottom of the screen, under the Computer subheading. To check your disk space, double-click the My Computer icon on your Desktop, then right-click the icon for your hard drive, and choose Properties. Your drive statistics will be shown there, including the amount of used and free hard-disk space.

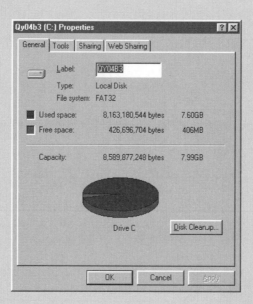

Question: Does WebSite Complete work with other operating systems?

Answer: At this time, there is neither a Macintosh nor a Linux version of WebSite Complete.

The basic system requirements include the following:

⬧ operating system: Windows 95/98/Me or Windows NT 4.0/ Windows 2000

⬧ RAM: 16MB for Windows 95/98; 32MB for Windows NT 4.0, Windows 2000, and Windows Me

- ❖ hard disk: at least 16MB free minimum for downloaded version, at least 65MB for CD-ROM version

- ❖ video: 16 colors minimum, 256 colors recommended

- ❖ CD-ROM drive: required for CD-ROM version installation and changes

- ❖ sound card: recommended, not required

- ❖ Web browser: Microsoft Internet Explorer (IE) version 5.0 or later (Microsoft Internet Explorer 5.5 is included under the Bonus Software on the included CD, or it can be downloaded from Microsoft's site at www.microsoft/com/ie) required for creating the Web sites only

- ❖ online access through an Internet Service Provider

These are indeed the minimum system requirements. Most Windows 95/98 or Windows Me users will feel more comfortable if they have at least 64MB of RAM. Also, at least 100MB of available disk space should always be available on the drive for the **Windows swap file** to operate.

Windows swap file
part of the Windows operating system that uses some of your hard-disk space as a virtual work space in which applications and data can be moved on and off the Desktop rapidly

Before Installing

It is always wise to close all other applications on your Windows Desktop before you begin installing a new software package. This not only frees up system resources, but it also reduces the chance that an installation problem will affect other applications open on the Desktop. For example, you wouldn't want to lose a document you're working on in another window if the install locks up the system and rebooting is your only option.

Be aware that some programs are more likely than others to interfere with software installation. Most notable of these is virus-scanning (also called antivirus) software, although some disk monitors and crash-protection programs do this, too. While it's good to be as protected as possible against file contamination by a virus, it's usually just as wise to turn off your **virus-scanning software** before you try installing programs such as WebSite Complete. You can turn the virus scanner back on after the install and allow the antivirus program to scan for any bad files that may have been introduced into your system. Check the Help menu of your antivirus software for instructions on temporarily disabling it.

virus-scanning software
also called antivirus software; designed to check your system for the presence of potentially harmful computer viruses that can affect the way your programs and/or your hardware performs

Also, if you haven't done so recently, it's probably a smart idea to perform disk maintenance prior to installing any large application. This can help an application install faster and run a bit faster because it will install to a better-organized hard-disk filing system. ScanDisk and Defrag are the two utilities provided in Windows to do this. These utilities, respectively, scan the hard disk for problems and try to repair them, then reorganize the hard-disk space by grouping the used space together.

How often these tools should be used depends on how much you use your PC. A good rule of thumb for a busy PC is to run them once a week, although ScanDisk will run automatically each time Windows shuts down improperly due to a crash or a lockup. For example, I usually run them just before I leave my office for the night so the time they take to run doesn't interfere with my work.

Installing WebSite Complete 4.0

Now that you've taken the steps necessary to help insure a good installation and checked your PC against the software's system requirements, you can proceed with the WebSite Complete setup. If you decide not to run ScanDisk and Defrag or shut down other software running on your system and you encounter a problem during WebSite Complete's installation, you should go back and do those things.

Before you start, remember to close any other applications on your Desktop. Then follow these steps:

1. Insert the WebSite Complete CD into your CD-ROM drive tray and close the drive tray. The software should automatically run (provided you haven't disabled the Auto Run of CDs).

   Or, go to Windows ➢ Start ➢ Run, click the Browse button to browse to the CD drive, and double-click Setup.

2. From the menu, choose Install WebSite Complete, which brings you to a Welcome screen.

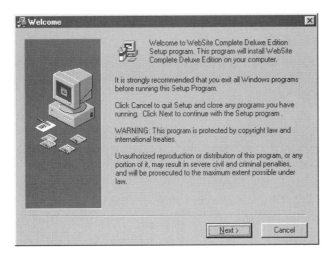

Click Next, then Next again.

3. From the Choose Destination Location window, choose where to install WebSite Complete. By default, this is the C:\...\WebSiteComplete Deluxe Edition folder, but you can click Browse to make another choice on your hard drive.

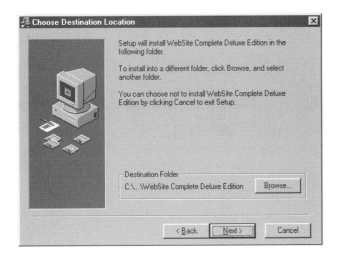

Click Next to continue.

4. Choose the name of the Program Manager group in which to place WebSite Complete. By default, WebSite Complete sets itself up in a new group called Go Daddy Software. Click Next, and then click Next again, which commences the install. Be patient, because the beginning of the installation, as files are copied, can move very slowly.

5. Once you see "Updating system configuration," the software has been successfully installed. Click Finish.

When the installation is complete, the initial WebSite Complete screen returns, offering you three options, as shown here:

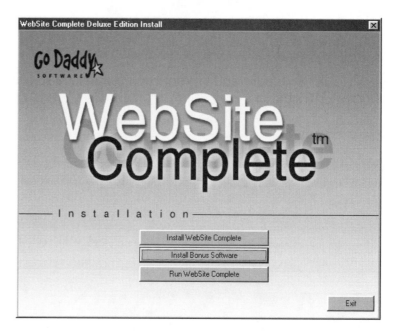

◇ Install WebSite Complete: you've already done this

◇ Install Bonus Software: more about this in the next section

◇ Run WebSite Complete: loads the software for the first time

Choose the operation you want to perform, or click Exit to close the installation window (you can rerun it at a later time, if desired).

Installing Bonus Software

WebSite Complete 4.0 includes bonus software that you can use later when working on your Web site, or use personally or professionally aside from the Web site. The bonus software includes the following packages:

◇ TaxACT 2000: tax preparation software

◇ Classic Fonts: a collection of fonts to add to your currently selected Windows application fonts, for possible use in your Web site design

- ❖ WordWeb: a Windows dictionary and thesaurus that can be used to check spelling and grammar

- ❖ eSafe Protect: antivirus software

- ❖ Internet Explorer 5.0: Microsoft's popular Web browser software required for the design of your Web site

- ❖ RealPlayer® 7.0: an Internet radio/audio player from RealNetworks® software (note: there is a more recent version available)

- ❖ RealProducer® 8: a radio/audio production program, also from RealNetworks® software

- ❖ Adobe® Acrobat® e Book Reader™: a reader for viewing Adobe PDF files, which are popular on various technical Web sites, as well as government Web sites such as the U.S. Internal Revenue Service

These extra packages are optional, so you can choose to install them or not. WebSite Complete will fully function with or without them, with one exception: Internet Explorer 5.0.

Follow these steps to install the bonus programs during your installation of WebSite Complete:

1. Once WebSite Complete finishes installing, choose Install Bonus Software from the Install window.

2. When you are presented with the list of bonus software to install, click to uncheck any software titles you do not wish to install (by default, they are all checked).

   You can click Cancel if you decide to bail out of installing any of the bonus packages.

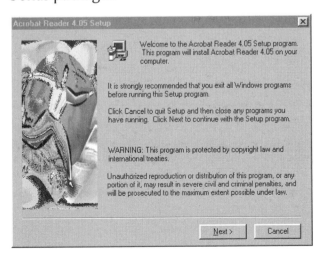

3. Click Next. Installation of the selected packages now begins.

Warning

Check your Start/Programs menu before installing any components of the bonus software to see if you already have one or more of the programs installed. It's always possible that you currently have a newer version installed than exists on the WebSite Complete CD, and you don't want to replace a newer version with a previous one.

If you opt not to install the bonus software but want to do so at another time, just locate your WebSite Complete CD and rerun as detailed above. Easier still is to use Windows Explorer to look at the contents of the CD, locate the program (such as IESetup or Acrobat Reader) on the CD, and click to install it directly.

Coping with Install Problems

Should you encounter problems installing Website Complete, follow these steps:

1. Close the WebSite Complete 4.0 Install window.

2. Close any other applications that are open on your computer.

3. Shut down and restart your PC.

4. Once Windows reloads, press Ctrl+Alt+Delete *once* to bring up Windows Task Manager (don't press it twice, or you restart your PC again).

5. In Task Manager, select each program or utility and click End Task until you are left with just Explorer and SysTray in the list.

6. If you failed to do so already, run your ScanDisk and Defrag utilities.

7. Repeat the steps for installing WebSite Complete.

If you're still having a problem, write down any error messages you receive. Then visit the Go Daddy Software support site at http://www.supportWebsite.com, using the account you usually use to access the Internet. Once there, you can browse messages from other users as well as post your own questions.

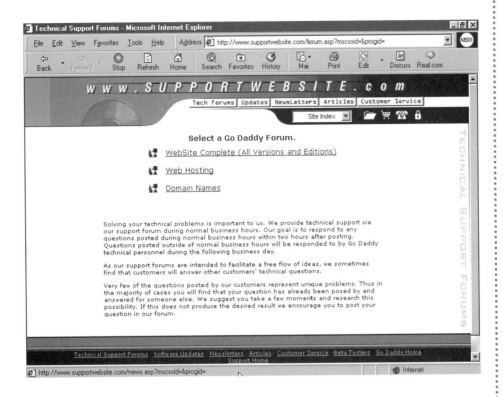

Launching WebSite Complete

In this section, you will learn how to launch WebSite Complete, get a taste of what WebSite Complete looks like, and learn what to do when first setting up a business Web site. You won't actually build your business site until Chapter 4, "Building Your First E-Commerce Web Site," but you'll want to acquaint yourself with the necessary information and how it gets plugged into the site before then.

In the steps covered here, you're going to end up with a basic beginning Web site that will probably look much better than one you might have made after a week or two with some fat books on HTML. While looks aren't everything, they really mean a great deal in a graphical environment like the World Wide Web. On the Web, visitors experience the overall look of your site before they begin digging into the actual content, which includes the products and services, your business information, and any articles, newsletters, or quick tips you may add. Sadly, the best content in the world tends not to get read by most visitors.

If you still have your WebSite Complete 4.0 Install window open, you can simply choose Run WebSite Complete to launch the program. If you've already closed it, follow these steps:

1. From Windows ➢ Start ➢ Programs, select Go Daddy Software.

2. From Go Daddy's submenu, choose WebSite Complete Deluxe Edition.

Once the software loads, you're ready to begin customizing your information and choosing the basic look and feel of your site.

Supplying Information

Once WebSite Complete loads for the first time, you are presented with a Welcome screen. Here you will supply the basic information required for WebSite Complete to help you build your site.

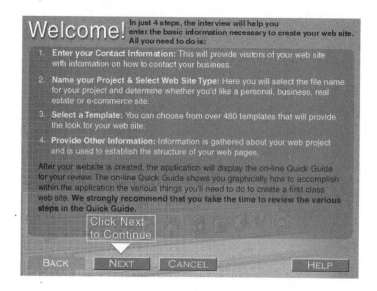

Four major setup steps are summarized on the Welcome screen:

❖ Your contact information gives the details necessary for visitors to contact you for further information or help.

❖ The name of the project determines the filename for the site you're producing, and your choice of a Web site type (business or personal, real estate or e-commerce/online store) determines the site design.

♦ You can choose a template from a set of designs offered in the software.

♦ You must also give additional types of information needed by WebSite Complete to begin putting the basics of your site together.

To proceed with the setup, follow these steps:

1. Click Next from the Welcome screen.

2. From the Contact Information screen, provide the following data:

♦ International Address: click Yes or No

♦ Web Site Name: type the name you choose for your Web site

♦ Person to Contact: type the name of the person in charge of the Web site, usually you

♦ Address (2 fields): type the physical street address of the contact person

♦ City

♦ State/Province

♦ Zip Code

♦ Phone Number

♦ Fax Number

♦ Second Phone (number)

♦ E-Mail: usually tied to the address of the Web site, but can be a reliable, alternate e-mail address

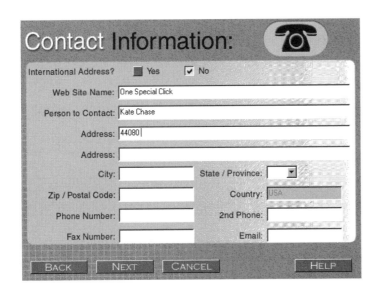

3. Click Next.

4. On the Name Your Project screen, the name of the Web site you entered on the Contact Information screen is provided in the Name field; edit as needed.

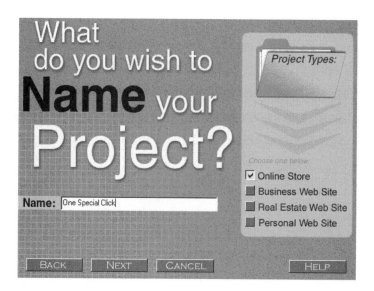

5. On the right side of the screen under Project Types, click to check Online Store and then click Next.

6. From the Web Site Information window, click to choose or type in the following data (you can check more than one option):

⬥ For My Company Offers, click to choose from Products (to sell goods), Services (to sell specific services), and/or Other (if neither of the other two apply).

⬥ For My Company Emphasizes, click to choose from Quality, Customer Support, and/or Affordable Pricing.

⬥ For Your Company Tagline (Motto), type your firm's motto, if applicable.

⬥ For Brief Description, type in a short summary of what your business does by completing the sentence "My company provides…"

⬥ For the Year Established, type in the year your business began or was founded.

⬥ For Founded By, type in the name of your business's founder.

7. Check the information supplied under Current Web Site Settings. If these are incorrect, click the Back button until you reach the screen with the wrong information, change it, and go back through the steps. Click Next.

Selecting a Template

What happens next may be a new concept to some: the use and selection of **templates**. Think of a template as a sort of blank form (or in this case, a blank Web page) that already has the background laid out for you and awaits any customization you may want to make. Lots of restaurants use templates to create their menus: The graphics and layout are already in place, and the menu selections and pricing need to be filled in. The use of templates can seriously cut down site-development time because you're using someone else's design to do some of the work. By selecting the best template for your needs, you can forego worrying about how to make the Web page look good and instead focus on the content of that page (information about your business and the goods and/or services you offer).

WebSite Complete comes with more than 480 Web templates. They are divided into various categories, many of which are suitable for an e-commerce site: Accounting, Business & Professional; Antiques, Arts & Crafts; Appliances; Books & News; Clothing, Jewelry & Accessories; Computers & Software; Gift Shops; Grocery; Real Estate & Homes; Restaurants & Bars; and so on.

Return now to the setup of WebSite Complete where you left off earlier once you clicked Next in step 7. Doing so brings up the Select a Template window.

1. In the top-right corner, scroll the drop-down list next to Categories to choose from a large list of professional and/or business categories, including those above.

2. For the selected category, you'll see two template options, but there are usually more templates with different graphics and page layouts. Use the horizontal scroll bar to move back and forth between the templates available in a given category. Double-click any of the templates to select it.

3. Click Customize a Template to create your own unique template. (This is the same option you get if you choose Customizable from the Template

templates
blank Web page forms in which you can add text and images based upon the layout provided

35

Categories list box. What's different here is that colors and graphics are not built into the custom templates; you add them later as you begin working on the basic Web site in Chapter 4.)

4. Click Download Templates to obtain templates online (not necessary if you have the CD) that you can use for site building. You'll need to be connected to the Internet for this, but the software will take you to the proper site for downloading the templates so you don't have to go hunting.

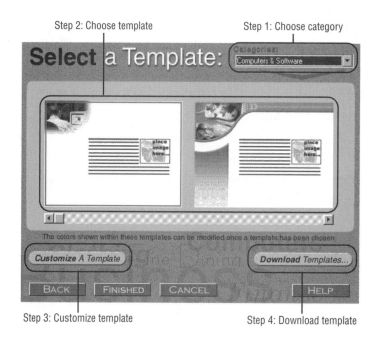

Step 2: Choose template   Step 1: Choose category

Step 3: Customize template   Step 4: Download template

Once you've chosen a template, click OK. A window will appear, reporting that the software is taking the information you supplied earlier and applying it to the template you just selected ("Applying New Template").

First Look at WebSite Complete

This brings you to the moment you've been waiting for: your first look at Web-Site Complete's design interface, as shown on the next page.

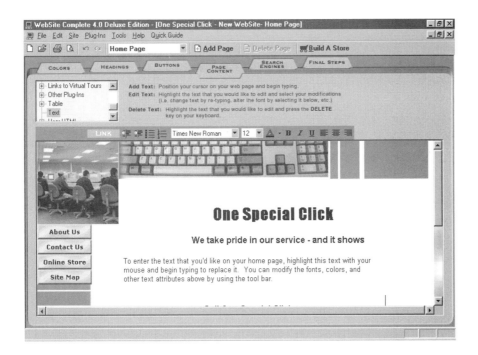

Feel free at this point to explore and play, but realize that you won't get into the actual work of designing the site until after you've planned it out in the next chapter. A professional Web site, particularly one offering goods and/or services, requires careful planning, even with all the supportive assistance WebSite Complete provides.

But if you're aching to jump ahead a little, a good place to start is the supplied Quick Guide that pops up each time you create a new Web site. Click the drop-down list to the right of Select a Topic to choose from mini tutorials on subjects such as adding audio files, working with Flash animations, and setting up an online store.

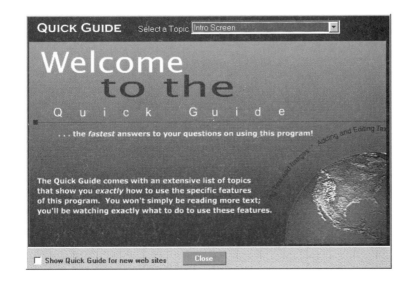

Then click Close whenever you want to return to WebSite Complete's main design window. You can reopen it at any time by clicking the Quick Guide option on the main design window's menu bar.

Chapter 3

Planning Your First E-Commerce Site

Good Web sites of any kind involve good planning and a good execution. Adding an e-commerce component to a site dramatically increases the need for good planning and organization. An e-commerce site requires a healthy application of logic, eye-pleasing design, functional ordering tools, and a true desire to sell goods and/or services. Any one of these alone wouldn't be nearly as effective for an online store as using all of them in tandem.

But before you sit down to begin planning your e-commerce site, you have to look at the whole project from two distinct vantage points: one as an entrepreneur trying to sell a product or service and the other as your customers seeing the site. Think about what you want them to see first when they visit your site. How easily can they find what you want to sell to them? Once they find what they're looking for, does your product or service information give them enough details to feel comfortable ordering? How readily can they locate like products? Since you're building the site, you know how to find things you've published to it. The visitor, on the other hand, needs directions. Keep these two vantage points in mind as you make your choices.

Planning Your Site's Look and Feel

Your site will differ from the rest by both its function and its overall look and feel. A site where people may order computer equipment is likely to have a theme that reflects the subject matter: a modern or futuristic appearance, images of various types of PC equipment, and technical information or online help for visitors looking to make a purchase. A gourmet food site might have a more whimsical atmosphere with warm colors, pictures of food or food preparation, softer fonts, and more flowery language to "romance" the visitor into purchasing the goods.

The Don'ts of E-Commerce Site Design

Can you guess the most common and destructive mistake that novice Web site designers make? You don't need to be a Web design specialist to figure this out. When you browse the Web (and you should definitely spend some time doing this before going too far in the design process), notice some of the details of the worst sites you see. Then ask yourself which elements of these sites make them unappealing to you:

- ❖ Are there "noisy" colors or annoying music playing endlessly?

- ❖ Is the print hard to read?

- ❖ Is everything jammed into the pages, or is it a big page with almost nothing on it?

- ❖ Is it difficult to find what you want?

- ❖ Are the instructions inadequate or missing?

- ❖ Do the pages look dated, or are there missing links to other pages?

- ❖ Are there options that don't work or buttons that fail to respond?

If some or all of these apply, these Web sites are indeed victims of the most common mistake: poor planning and implementation. Sometimes bad design happens because designers are in a hurry to get their site up and running, and they leave things that they think they will fix later but then don't. Sometimes it happens because newer Web designers want to include every cool feature from spinning icons and shimmering colors to dynamic pictures, loud sound files that loop over and over, and lots of special effects. While designers of personal Web sites are more susceptible to these mistakes, they are also seen in the commercial realm. The sample "bad" page below is a re-creation of a site for a furniture store with a very frustrating order page.

In fact, you can spend less than 20 minutes on the Web and find five examples of online sales sites where the goods and/or services are so buried beneath the special effects that it feels more like a trip to Disneyland than a trip to buy products (see the example of the re-created site on the next page). Two of these five sites also have Order Here! buttons that do absolutely nothing. That's obviously not the impression a successful e-commerce site wants to give.

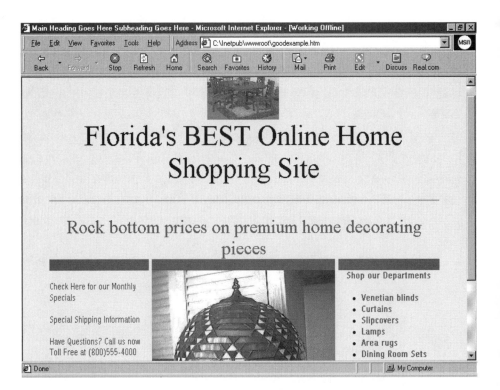

Some of the more effective small business sites find it far more useful to let the products or packages, rather than the background artwork, dazzle the consumer.

You must assume that visitors to your site will be there to get what they need—information to consider when choosing a product or service if not yet the purchase itself—and leave. You can offer stunning graphics, tips, surveys, feedback functions (so customers can let you know what they think of your site), and animations to enhance your site, but you should never make the potential customer hunt through a mass of screens and distractions to find the very thing you're selling.

The Do's of E-Commerce Site Design

By choosing to use WebSite Complete, you remove much of the difficulty and concern. By using the wide selection of templates available in the software (discussed in the previous chapter), you can plug the components of your site into a well-designed model rather than design a site and all its associated pages from the ground up. As much as possible, the templates help you hit the important "do" list for a commercial Web site, while limiting the number of "don'ts" you can apply. But you still need to make certain that the components you plug into the template meet your needs as a vendor and a visitor's needs as a potential consumer.

The list below represents some of the very basic rules that you, as a beginning Web site creator, should follow as you use WebSite Complete to prepare your site and then augment it with features that make it uniquely your own:

- ✧ Keep it simple. You can add bells and whistles, but be sure that anything you do on your Web site will be easy for your visitors to follow and understand; make your most important products and information easy to locate.

- ✧ Keep it focused and professional. You should include what you think is necessary and exclude what's unnecessary. For example, your commercial Web site might include an image of a group of workers at your business, but it probably shouldn't include photos of your friends, your family, or your pets; personal, political, or religious statements; or promotions for distinctly unrelated material.

- ✧ Know your content. Don't include any content or articles that you haven't read thoroughly, and make certain you have permission to use any content you get from an outside source (don't reprint articles from newspapers or magazines, for example, without proper permission).

- ✧ Emphasize customer service and support. If your small business or company values its customers, show it on your Web site. Offer extra help and instruction where needed, give shoppers ways to contact you if they encounter a problem with the site or its service, and make the tone of your text reflect the customer commitment you have.

- ✧ Keep reviewing the site. A good Web site is one that has other sets of eyes check it for usability and readability before it goes live on the Internet, and one that is maintained properly so that faulty options are fixed quickly.

Elements and Pages WebSite Complete Provides for You

WebSite Complete sets up the structure of various basic elements for you, including a roster of commonly used pages for commercial Web sites. These include the following:

- ✧ The Home page is the main entry page for the Web site to which every other page is linked directly or indirectly.

❖ The About Us page gives basic information about your business or company.

❖ The Contact Us page lists ways to contact your business or company.

❖ The Online Store page is the entry page into product shopping.

❖ The Customer Login page is used for customers to register with your site by using a name and password and then return by logging in with that name and password. This feature lets you know who your customers are and how often they check back.

❖ The Product List page offers a listing of products (or services) available on your site.

❖ The Shopping Cart page is used for holding your customers' purchase orders until the checkout procedure so that they don't have to check out after selecting each item in a multiple-item order.

❖ The Your Account page gives information about customer accounts, usually only found on sites that require (or request) that visitors register (may give order-tracking options, a listing of past orders, or basic ship-to or payment information).

❖ The Product page contains basic information on each product offered.

❖ The Site Map page lays out your site.

❖ The Listings page—only available on real estate–selected sites—produces property listings visitors can browse.

If you want to add more pages to your site, you simply use the Add a Page tool that will be discussed in the next chapter.

Before Building Your Site

Here's a list of the types of files and information you should have available as you build your e-commerce site, depending on your specific needs:

❖ your business logo (if applicable), which you'll insert as an image wherever you want it to appear, usually stored in JPG or GIF format

- company info (sometimes called About Us) that can be built or copied from a text file and used to provide basic information about your business or online store (who runs it, when it was founded, special accomplishments)

- various contact methods (e-mail, phone, fax, or store location) that customers can use to reach you if they have a question or experience a problem with their order

- shopping details that describe how to place orders for goods or services, how long it may take for the customer to receive the order, and what payment methods you allow

- shipping information, which supplies details about available shipping methods, shipping costs, and any shipping restrictions

- organization of content for grouping and presenting products or services

- promotions that offer weekly specials or featured products

Other Considerations

There are many other elements that you can add to your business site, such as favorable reviews of your products or services or a listing of important clients. You can add a page for an Editor's Pick-of-the-Month to review a specific product. You can also create seasonal pages or have material for special occasions, as they relate to your business. For example, a small seed company might have an article with a set of tips for gardeners as they prepare their gardens in the fall, while a small clothing maker might feature tips on fabrics for keeping warm in winter or cool in summer, along with links to recommended products.

Keep a checklist of the features you may want to add to your e-business site after the first time you publish it. It will help you keep track of your bright ideas and items of special interest that you encounter on other e-business sites as you browse. You can customize and incorporate these ideas later, when you have a need and the time. Remember that a Web page isn't static. You can go back at any time and make changes. In fact, you should make changes periodically to keep the site's appearance fresh so that visitors know that the site is an active part of your business and that they will have your attention.

Tip

If your list gets too long, try organizing the items by priority under such categories as "Next Time," "Within the Next Month," and "Long Term."

Planning Your Product Presentations

How you present your products and/or services is vitally important. In fact, since WebSite Complete takes care of so much of your site setup, you can instead spend your time on deciding which products to present and how.

You must first decide which products or services you plan to sell on your site. Some Web-store entrepreneurs offer only a select number of products from their total inventory online, while others choose to sell some products exclusively on the Internet. Some limitations may be inherent based on product type; for example, not all products ship well, or may cost so much to ship in a special way (such as products that must stay very cold or those that are extremely delicate) that it really prices you out of offering them on the Internet.

Next you must decide how to describe your products or services. Descriptions of the products should be relatively short (usually no more than a few hundred words) but enticing. Make them too long, and there's a chance that visitors won't read them. Make them too short, and visitors may pass the product over because they feel they don't know enough about it to order. Use the same principles for the Web that you might in demonstrating a product or service for a physical audience, giving them good reason to buy what you have to sell while economizing the words used. Exercise care in getting your information right, and always check your spelling.

Where applicable, use graphics of the products or related to the services offered so that potential buyers have a good sense of what they're purchasing.

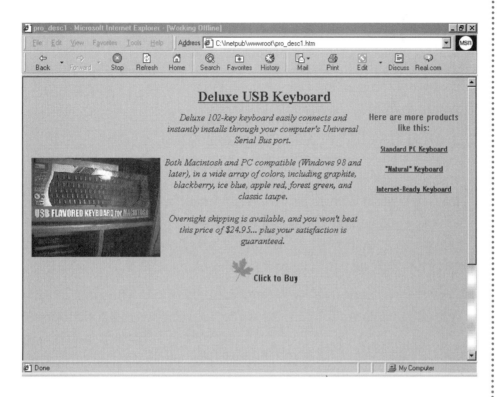

For obvious reasons, these graphics should be of the highest possible quality while still being small enough to load quickly. If visitors have to wait endlessly for large graphics to display, they're likely to give up and go elsewhere.

If you decide to offer a feature on your site, as most do, to allow for customer feedback or questions, you have to plan for how you will handle these communications. Internet customers tend to look for instant answers, so Web shopkeepers who take a week or two—or more—to respond may not get the sales a more responsive Web shop would. After all, customers want to believe that there are humans actually running the Web site behind the scenes; if they feel everything is automated, they may be concerned that there will be no system in place to deal with a problem with their order if one arises.

Typically, these feedback or contact mechanisms allow the visitor to fill out a short form, which is then submitted to you via e-mail. If the submitter's e-mail address is supplied, you can then reply directly to the customer.

Web host provider

an individual or company that rents out time, space, and services on its commercial servers so that individuals and small companies can have a Web-based presence and/or operation without having to have all of the hardware, software, and high-speed connections themselves

Choosing a Web Host

To publish your site, you must choose a Web host or **Web host provider**. By using a Web host provider, you're sharing the costs of running a commercial, always available professional Web server. By sharing, the monthly cost is much lower and more in line with what an individual businessperson or small company can afford.

You may ask why you can't just cut out the middleman and publish a Web site on your home or office computer and let people connect to you to access your Web site. After all, there are products, such as Microsoft FrontPage® and Microsoft Personal Web Server (PWS), that allow you to create a disk-based Web to which you can publish and share a site right off your hard drive. Depending on how you set this up, you can have just about all the basic functionality you'd have if setting up a formal Web site through a Web host provider.

However, for most uses—and particularly for those who want to set up an e-commerce Web site—this isn't a very practical way to go for several reasons. For one, by opening your PC so that others can access your disk-based Web, you're jeopardizing your PC's own security. Depending on how you've set up your own system for security, the possibility exists that others may have access to more than your Web site, such as credit card information and work files.

Warning

If you've been on the Internet for a bit, you may have heard of, or even installed, something called a firewall. What a firewall on a PC does is try to restrict others from accessing your PC while you're connected to the Internet and prevent certain information sharing, based on security levels you set. If you decide to install a firewall on your PC, check the documentation first to see if it provides any information on using the product in conjunction with Web publishing. Some PC firewall programs, when set to extremely secure settings, may interfere with the Web-publishing process.

Tip

If you have a firewall and are in doubt about whether it may cause a problem with publishing, you may want to temporarily disable your firewall program before you upload your site for the first time. Or you can try publishing with the firewall turned on, and then disable it only if you have a problem.

Another reason to forego disk-based Webs is that most people don't have a dedicated connection to the Internet, so the disk-based Web would only be available when you're logged on to the Internet, and it would be difficult for people to find you. It would be slow for them to access you, too, because of your connection. Finally, you wouldn't be operating a World Wide Web site, just a Web off your hard disk. So you could forget easy financial transactions or any of the extras a product such as WebSite Complete provides to make it easy for you to set up and publish to a Web host provider.

Another question some ask is why they can't use some of the free Web hosting services available on the Internet, such as NBCi.com, or the small amount of free space for a Web site that some ISPs make available as part of having an account with them.

In these situations, you'll have to read the Terms of Use agreement such services provide to see whether commercial transactions—where you're selling products or services from your "free" site—are allowed. You'll find very few completely free Web providers who permit you to do commercial sales. For one, they're geared toward making creative personal space available to individuals who, for example, want to publish a few pages about their family or a special interest or who want to share their writing or photographs. For another, even a small business can generate a lot of traffic and capacity demands that exceed the **bandwidth** of these sites. If the free service is going to have to work extra hard to provide access to your site, it will want to charge you to do so.

bandwidth
overall connection capability

Tip

If you find a free service to host your Web site, you won't have what's needed to develop your online store using WebSite Complete.

Also, these services don't typically let you use a **domain name**. What you often get stuck using is a rather long, elaborate, and very hard-to-remember Web address or URL (Universal Resource Locator) that serves as a sort of street address for your Web site. People aren't likely to remember these long Web site addresses off the top of their heads, so they'll have to have a link to connect to it. If they don't have a link available, they may not find you and that's contraindicated for good sales.

domain name
the registered name of a Web site

Finally, even if you could set up an online store on a freebie host, you probably wouldn't like the overall experience for all the reasons stated above and more.

For example, most of these sites aren't set up to automate the publishing of your site, so you may have to upload everything page by page, picture by picture. If you're a small business owner, you probably don't have the time for these extra steps, and you appreciate anything that can save you some precious time.

Considering Cost and Software

The monthly fee for hiring a Web host provider depends on the level of service required. Many small businesses need just basic service, running anywhere from $10–50 per month plus add-on fees for having the Web host provider handle the financial transactions on their system.

One important question to answer before choosing a Web host provider is whether the software you want to use is compatible with the way they want you to set up your Web site. For example, Go Daddy Software, the makers of WebSite Complete, offers Web hosting at a highly competitive price. (Whether you choose Go Daddy as a provider or not, you must choose one that supports the Go Daddy Web approach so that all of the features and functions will be available to you and your work will be easier.)

Another key factor in your choice of a Web host relates directly to online transactions. Not all small vendors are set up to take credit cards for payment, since it requires a private arrangement with a financial institution or card company. Because customers usually pay for their online orders by credit card, this is an important consideration.

Note

There are some companies providing intermediary services—where a customer opens an online account of sorts, deposits funds into it, and then draws against that account when they make an online purchase—as an alternative to taking credit cards for payment. At the time of the writing of this book, however, most of these companies are fledgling at best, and the practice is still not widely accepted. But this may change. Some customers resist giving sensitive credit card and personal information over the computer. Also, it is expected that the Internet will expand to accept a broader range of users who either choose not to use credit or may not be eligible for a credit card account. Innovations usually come at the behest of demand.

Choosing a Domain Name for Your E-Business

A domain name is the name of a particular Web site. Internet addresses, by nature, aren't name driven, but refer to a specific IP (Internet Protocol) address, like 208.132.195.33. Because a string of numbers is difficult to remember, the domain name convention is used to assign easy names to a Web site. To reach my professional Web site, for example, you could type its IP address (**http://208.132.195.53**) into your Web browser or, to do it more easily, you can type in **http://www.reluctanttech.com**. The "reluctanttech" in www.reluctanttech.com is the actual domain name. The "www" refers to the World Wide Web, and the part after the domain (in this case, ".com") is the identifying suffix.

Including Domain Suffixes

These are some of the suffixes currently in use (although the Internet governing bodies are in the process of adding more, including ".biz" for business and ".info" for information-based sites):

> .cc for commercial companies
>
> .com for commercial businesses
>
> .edu for educational organizations
>
> .gov for government agencies and offices
>
> .mil for military organizations
>
> .net for network organizations
>
> .org for nonprofit organizations

Note

There are now five more suffixes approved (in addition to .biz and .info) by the ICANN (International Corporation of Assigned Names and Numbers). They include the following: .name (for registering your name), .pro (for professionals such as doctors), .museum (self-explanatory), .aero (for airplanes and the aero industry), and .coop (for cooperatives). These *should* all be in place by the summer of 2001.

Typically, a commercial Web site will choose to run its main business site from a domain address with either a `.com` or `.net` suffix since those are the best known and most widely used. Sometimes a business will choose to register domains with more than one suffix type.

Registering Your Domain

You can't just make up a domain name and start using it. What if someone else is using it? You have to register a domain with one of the companies licensed with special Internet authorities by paying a fee (often an annual fee of $8–35) and filling out basic information about who runs the site, as shown below. Once registered, you then have the right to use that domain name until you either sell it or stop paying for its reregistration, which needs to be done once a year (or longer, if your domain registrar allows you to pay for multiple years at a time, usually at a slight discount). In a situation like that with WebSite Complete, you need only to register the domain and then give it to your Web host. The host can then take care of a lot of the details for you in making the site live with that domain name.

One of the reasons against going with a free Web hosting company is that you often can't use your own domain name. You're usually stuck with a long Web address that may not point to anything a visitor can readily identify as you and your business. If you have a company called One Special Click, imagine how much easier it would be to have visitors find `www.onespecialclick.com` than something like `www.freespacehere.net/companies/nereg/stores/onespecialclick.asp`.

Deciding on a Domain Name

Selecting a good domain name isn't always the kind of thing you can do in five minutes. For one, you have an incredible amount of competition for more common names or very descriptive names. As I write this, just under 29 million domain names are currently registered, so you may find it helpful to come up with a list of 15–20 possibilities before you begin to check for available names. Some entrepreneurs have made a game out of letting existing customers suggest names for their Web site domain. Others enlist the creative aid of friends, colleagues, and family members in making their selection.

Even though the competition for good names can be pretty aggressive and thousands of new domains are registered globally each day, you should probably give yourself at least 24 hours to "live" with the name before you register it. Test it out on friends and colleagues. Then register it.

Here are other important considerations when selecting a domain name for your online venture:

- ◇ Make it fit your business. If your actual business name is already taken, try to get as close as you can to the overall nature of your business.

- ◇ Keep it simple. The longer and more difficult the name, the more likely that visitors will have a hard time finding you.

- ◇ Avoid word plays. Don't try to play off a better-known business' name. It could backfire and cause you to get a letter from the business' attorney, and it may not even help your sales.

◇ Set up multiple registrations. You can register the domain name for more than one identifying category, thus using your business name with the same basic domain name and different suffixes (onespecialclick.com, onespecialclick.net, onespecialclick.cc, etc.). This reduces the chance that a like business will set up shop with the same domain but a different suffix and cost you shoppers.

Tip

You can also use multiple registrations to secure domain names that are close to the spelling of your domain or common misspellings of that name. This way, if a potential customer misspells your domain, you "own" that misspelling and can set up a page to direct them to your real Web site. You would only manage the main site. You can "park" the other domain registrations with your Web host. Of course, you should check with your Web host first to see if they offer free or low-cost parking of domain names for their customers.

Warning

Internet authorities—and courts—are cracking down on the phenomenon of *cybersquatting*, or the practice of registering and keeping the domain name of someone else's product or business "on hold" with the purpose of getting that person or business to pay a large sum of money to obtain it.

Checking for Domain Availability

Follow these steps to check for the availability of the domain name you wish to register:

1. While you're logged into the Internet and with your Web browser loaded, type the following address in your address bar: **http:// www.whois.net**.

2. Once on the site, go to the dialog box to the right of Search by Domain Name or by Keyword and click Go. This starts a search to determine whether or not the domain name (or any of its variants by different suffixes) is available.

3. Repeat as necessary until you find an acceptable domain name.

You can perform the same search on Go Daddy Software's Web site (and on a host of other **domain registration** and Web host companies). Here's how you do it with Go Daddy:

domain registration
the act of registering a Web site name with an authorized registering agent

1. While you're logged into the Internet and with your Web browser loaded, type the following address in your address bar: **http:// www.godaddy.com**.

2. Once on the site, look for the Domain Search box and type in the domain name you want to search.

3. To the right of this, click the suffix type you want (.com, .net, etc.) from the drop-down list. Click Go. A page will display the search results, telling you whether or not the domain is available.

4. Repeat as necessary.

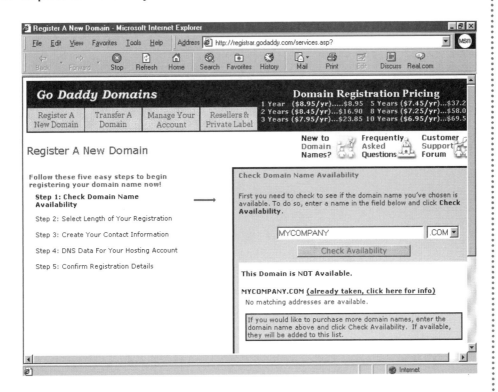

Once you find a name, you need to go through the process of registering it. This process differs slightly, depending on where you register your site. If you do it when you sign up for a Web host, you may have to fill out a separate screen for domain registration, or you may have to answer any necessary registration questions as part of the Web host sign-up process.

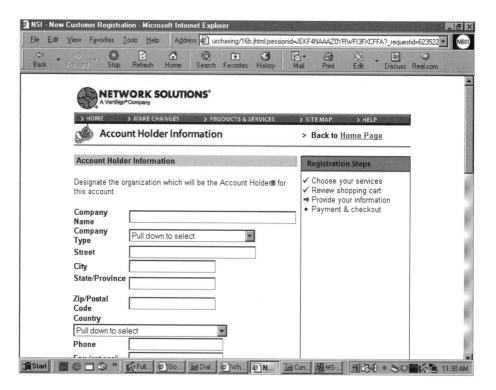

Chapter 4

Building Your First E-Commerce Web Site

Now that you know some Web and Internet basics, have a brief introduction to the world of e-commerce, can install the WebSite Complete software, and have at least a rough idea of what you want to include on your first e-business site, it's time to put all that information together to build your site. At this stage, don't worry about making mistakes or having your first efforts not come out quite as you like. Until you publish your site to the Web through a Web host, your trials and errors are stored locally and available only on your hard drive. This means that just you or anyone else you allow to access your machine will see your efforts.

As you move through this chapter, you and WebSite Complete will build your first Web site project. You will then learn how to customize the site so that it's not only functional for offering products and services, but uniquely yours as well. While WebSite Complete offers the format and functions through its wizards, it also provides many options to modify the color and/or color scheme, change the font used for text or **buttons**, and add your own text and images.

buttons

Web site visitors click these navigational tools to link to a new page or tool

Supplying Information and Choosing a Template

You will now revisit the first few screens of WebSite Complete (you first saw them during installation in Chapter 2, "Getting Started with WebSite Complete 4.0"). You will go through these screens (information entry and selection of template) again, this time actually building your basic site.

1. From Windows Start ➢ Programs ➢ Go Daddy Software, choose Web-Site Complete Deluxe Edition to load the program.

2. From the Welcome screen, choose Next to move to the Contact Information field.

Note

If you've jumped ahead and started a Web site already, you'll be presented with a Welcome Back screen. From this screen, choose Start a New Web Site and click Next.

3. Fill in the contact information as you want it to appear (refer to Chapter 2, if necessary) and click Next.

4. On the left side of the Name Your Project screen, type in a name for your project (if it differs from your Web site name) in the Name field.

5. On the right side of the Name Your Project screen, choose the type of project you want this to be:

    ◇ Online Store for selling products

    ◇ Business Web Site for offering services

- ◆ Real Estate Web Site for handling realty services and sales information

- ◆ Personal Web Site for creating a strictly personal (noncommercial, nonprofessional) Web site

Then click Next.

Warning

If you choose the Personal Web Site option, go directly to step 7 to select a template.

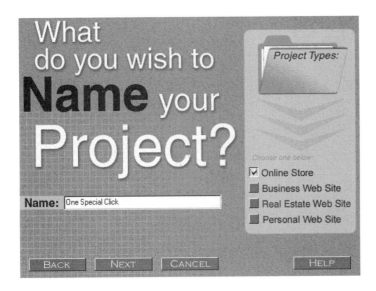

6. On the Web Site Information screen, provide or make a choice from the following:

- ◆ In the My Company Offers field, choose Products, Services, and/or Other (you can choose more than one, as applicable).

- ◆ In the My Company Emphasizes field, choose Quality, Customer Support, and/or Affordable Pricing (you can choose more than one).

- ◆ Type in your company's tagline or motto in the Your Company Tagline (Motto) field, if applicable.

- ◆ In the Brief Description field, finish the description that begins "My company provides…"

- ◆ Type in the appropriate four-digit year in the Year Established field.

◇ In the Founded By field, type in the name(s) of your company's founder(s).

Then click Next. A message will tell you that the software is building the template list based on your choices.

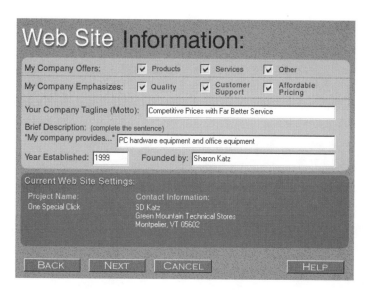

Web Site Information:

My Company Offers:	☑ Products	☑ Services	☑ Other
My Company Emphasizes:	☑ Quality	☑ Customer Support	☑ Affordable Pricing

Your Company Tagline (Motto): Competitive Prices with Far Better Service

Brief Description: (complete the sentence)
"My company provides..." PC hardware equipment and office equipment

Year Established: 1999   Founded by: Sharon Katz

Current Web Site Settings:

Project Name: Contact Information:
One Special Click   SD Katz
                       Green Mountain Technical Stores
                       Montpelier, VT 05602

| BACK | NEXT | CANCEL | HELP |

7. In the Select a Template screen, choose the category that best fits your business or service from the drop-down list at the top right.

8. Once you choose the category, templates for that category are lined up in the middle window of the same screen. Use the scroll bar to move left and right between choices. Click to select a template, and then click Finished.

Note

You'll also notice two other options in the Select a Template window: Customize a Template and Download Template. You'll learn about customizing your template later in this chapter, in the section titled "Customizing the Design of Your Site." You would use the Download Template option to view templates to consider before you settle on a design for your site.

When you click Finished, you'll see a pop-up window for the Quick Guide (refer to the section titled "First Look at WebSite Complete" in Chapter 2). Check this out for information and tips on using the software to create your site.

Now you've come to the main working screen of WebSite Complete. From here, you will take the format the software has built for you and begin plugging in your customized information and objects. Here begins your real work in establishing first the Web site's main page, also called home page, as well as the collection of other pages that you'll eventually publish to your Web site.

Working with the Main Screen

Because all of your options for both basic and customized WebSite Complete functions are available from the main screen, you should become familiar with it.

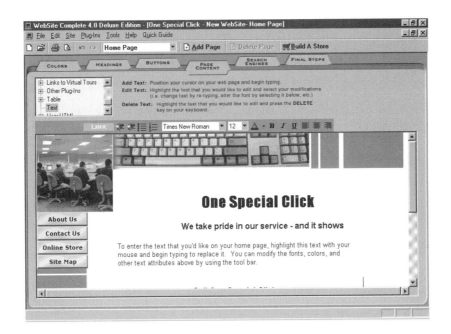

The screen is divided into parts. As with other Windows applications, the menu bar is at the top, with options such as File, Edit, and View. Below it is the icon-based toolbar, which offers options such as New, Open, Print, Preview Web, a drop-down list of pages, Add Page, Delete Page, and Build a Store (note the shopping cart).

Next comes the main working area of the page, which has a few major components. At the top is Control Panel with its tabs for manipulating specific options, and at the bottom is the working draft of your Web page.

Working from the Menu Bar

As with other applications, WebSite Complete's most critical functions are available on the menu bar. You'll find many of the key tools here, like Preview and Print, echoed in other aspects of the program such as the toolbar. It's a good idea to get to know these options immediately, so you won't have to stumble around to find a specific function later on. The key tools on the menu bar include the following:

❖ From the File option, you can choose to open, save, close, print, back up, or restore your project, and, very importantly, preview your site.

❖ The Edit option offers the regular Windows editing tools such as Cut, Copy, Paste, Undo, and Redo, plus other options such as Change Template, General Information (about your project), Show Borders, and Show Page Elements.

❖ With the Site option, you can choose various tools for working with your site, including the following:

   ❖ Page List provides a list of all pages you've created for your site.

Note

Does the page list seem longer than you expected? Depending on what type of site (online store, real estate, and so on) you select during setup, WebSite Complete has automatically added the pages it predicts you'll need. You can remove any of the additional pages besides your home page or add more pages to this basic list. More about this later in this chapter.

   ❖ Add Page creates a new page for your site.

   ❖ Delete Pages removes a page from your site.

   ❖ Rename Page renames an existing Web page on your site.

   ❖ Publish to the Internet helps you connect to the Internet (if you're not already online) to publish your site.

   ❖ Register with Search Engines helps you register your site with large Web-based Internet search engines.

❖ The Plug-Ins option allows you to add extra components to your Web site, such as a loan or property payment calculator for real estate listings, an event calendar, and Flash animations (covered in Chapter 5, "Adding Special Features to Your E-Commerce Web Site").

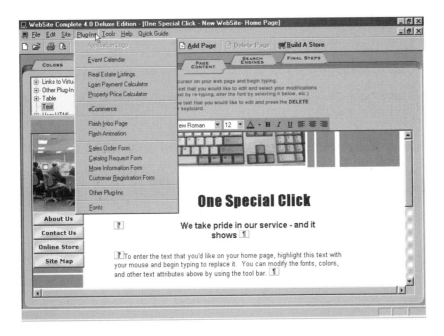

- ◇ The Help option allows you to check the online help.

- ◇ The Quick Guide loads WebSite Complete's bonus help guide, which shows you how to use specific functions or perform certain operations.

Working with the Toolbar

The toolbar stores the critical tools you may need to access quickly. These tools are often represented by a graphical button for quicker access.

The toolbar offers these options:

- ◇ Use New to create a new Web project.

- ◇ Use Open to open a Web project.

- ◇ Use Print to send a copy of the current page to the printer.

- ◇ Use Preview Web to see how your Web page will appear when published.

- ◇ Use Undo to remove the last change you made.

- ◇ Use Redo to replace the last change made.

◇ Use the Current Page listing to show the page title currently being worked on, with the option to switch to other pages in your Web using a drop-down menu.

◇ Use Add Page to help you add a new page to your Web site.

◇ Use Delete Page to help you remove a page from your Web site.

◇ Use Build Online Store to aid you in constructing an online shop to sell products.

Working with Control Panel

WebSite Complete's Control Panel is composed of three major areas. First, tabs labeled Colors, Headings, and so on are at the top. Each tab focuses on a specific function of creation or customization, such as Page Content or Buttons. Next, the options available under each tab are displayed in the middle of Control Panel, which is then bordered on the bottom by a formatting toolbar. This toolbar allows you to apply changes, add or modify graphics with the Image button, link to other pages, change the font properties, and justify the text or an image. This formatting bar appears only on views where font or justification is relevant, so, for example, you won't see it when you have the Search Engine tab selected.

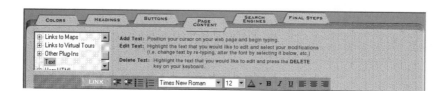

Control Panel tabs include the following:

◇ With the Colors tab, you can change the overall color scheme of the site from the drop-down palette, choose from the template colors on the right, or use Create Color Set to customize your page colors.

◇ With the Headings tab, you can add or modify headings that appear on the current page, or use the toolbar to change the heading font, font size, or appearance.

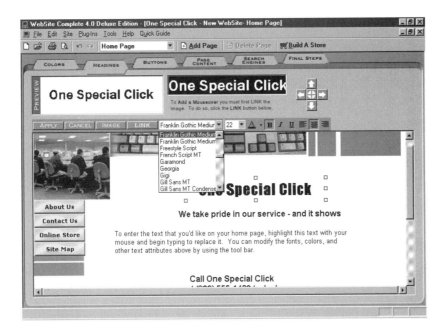

- The Buttons tab gives you the ability to add or change buttons or to modify the text that appears on them.

- The Page Content tab allows you to make modifications to the content of a page, such as the text that appears on it.

- The Search Engines tab permits you to set up keywords of subjects and names appearing on the site, which can then be used in Internet search engines such as AltaVista, Yahoo!, and Google.

- The Final Steps tab lets you automate the steps necessary to connect to your Web host and publish your site.

Working with the Page Layout

Below Control Panel is your page according to the company information and template selection that you provided in WebSite Complete. If you choose Online Store, for example, as your Web site type, you'll see that heading appear on the page.

In the example below, you'll see the name of the site, the artwork included automatically through the use of the chosen template, and several basic links available on the left side of the page. These links serve both to organize information you may want to include and to provide a navigational tool for visitors.

For instance, as a visitor moves off the home, or main, page of the site to other pages, the link labeled Home Page can easily return them where they started. These same links are echoed by the underlined hyperlinks, or links, at the bottom of the page (you may need to scroll down to see them).

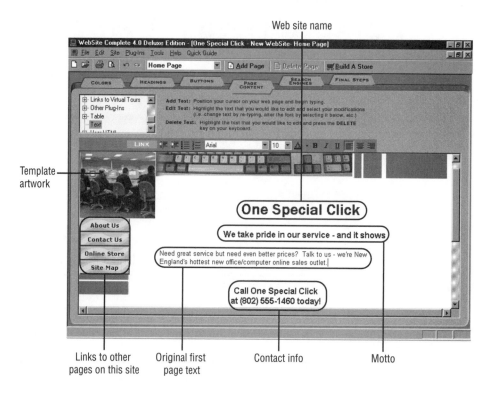

Web site name

Template artwork

Links to other pages on this site

Original first page text

Contact info

Motto

To begin working with any of these aspects of your Web page, just click the desired area. If you're not satisfied with how the general information that you first supplied now appears on the page, click the Site option on the menu bar and choose General Information. You can click any entry, retype it, and click OK.

Customizing the Design of Your Site

You now have a basic Web page. If you were planning to post a quick one-page site with informational text about your business, you'd practically be ready to publish. But you're building an e-commerce site, which requires more than the standard elements already plugged into your site. Your site also requires a degree of customized information about you, your business, and the goods or services it offers—and it needs to be ready to accept orders for those.

This section will prepare you to make the changes to this basic page that make it personally and professionally yours. Think of it as using a canvas on which someone has filled in some of the background, so now you don't have quite as much work to do.

Note

As you work, refer often to the detailed plans you made as you worked through Chapter 3, "Planning Your First E-Commerce Site," so that you don't forget to include any information or images. You may even want to use the checklist you created in that chapter to track exactly where you are in the master plan for your Web site project.

Modifying or Customizing Your Template

You may decide that you don't want to use the same template you first selected when you started this Web project. Or you may want to customize the template by changing its color scheme and/or background (a background here refers to the base look of the page behind the text and images). You may also want to have more say in deciding how and what text and images will appear in the template. This section will show you how to make common changes to your template.

Modifying the Template Color

You can modify the existing colors in your template's color scheme in one of two ways. The first involves creating a custom color set for the template, which you can accomplish by following these steps:

1. With the current Web project open, click the Colors tab in Control Panel.

2. Click the Create Color Set icon.

3. When prompted, type a name for your custom color set.

4. Choose the feature you wish to modify.

5. Select one of the listed colors, or click More to see additional choices or to create a truly custom color.

6. Repeat these changes until you're satisfied with the color set selected.

7. Click Save to save your color set.

8. Click Apply to apply the new color set to your template and return to the main screen.

If you're not looking for custom colors and just want to use a different color from the current one, perform these steps instead:

1. With the current Web project open, click the Colors tab in Control Panel.

2. Next to Change Colors, click to open the drop-down menu.

3. Select a color from the choices provided; the color change is immediately applied.

Modifying the Template Background

If you want to experiment with the effect of different background looks on the overall appearance of your Web template, follow these steps:

1. With the current Web project open, click the Colors tab in Control Panel.

2. Click Change Background.

3. Choose the background type you want to modify and click OK.

Customizing Your Template

You may want a template that offers a slightly different look or setup from those available from the prepared templates in WebSite Complete. Fortunately, the software allows you to take an essentially blank template and construct a customized template from it, using your own theme(s) and images. You can then use it as the basis for your site, just as you can with the prepared templates. To customize a template, follow these steps:

1. For a new Web project, load WebSite Complete and follow the steps for setting up a site. From the Select a Template window, choose Customize a Template.

Or, for replacing a template applied to an existing Web project, open the Web project in WebSite Complete, click the Colors tab in Control Panel, and then click the Change Template button.

2. Locate a satisfactory customizable template design and click it. Click OK. A window will pop up very briefly letting you know that the new template is being applied.

3. From the page view, double-click the image place marker (you may have more than one) on your page template.

4. From the resulting Customize a Template window, select the image you wish to use and use the associated image controls to position the image as you want it to appear. Click OK.

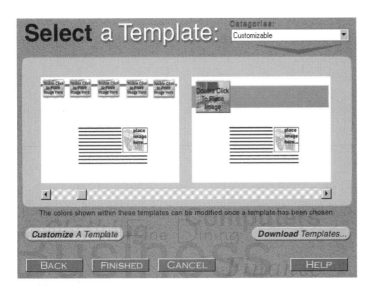

Replacing the Template

You may find yourself wondering if you've made the best possible template choice for building your Web site. Or you may just want to continue experimenting with how certain features work against different templates. These are the steps to follow to replace one template with another:

1. From WebSite Complete and with your current Web project open, click the Colors tab in Control Panel.

2. Click the Change Template button.

3. Choose the replacement template you want to try and click OK.

The new template you have chosen will then immediately replace your previous template.

Adding and Changing Text

A certain amount of default text—particularly for labels and links on the site—is supplied by WebSite Complete as it builds your initial project. Depending on your particular needs, much of this may be suitable to use as is, but you should review it as you work and make any necessary or desired changes.

Keep these Web text rules in mind as you work:

1. Be friendly and inviting in your tone.

2. Use an intelligent economy of words: Convey your message in as few words as reasonably possible. Web site visitors are often reluctant to read large blocks of text.

3. Keep your audience in mind: The language you would use to sell gourmet food may differ a lot from the language you would use to sell specialty parts.

4. Use images—where needed—to enhance your message.

5. Watch the font types and colors you use: Some may be more difficult to read than others; black text in a common font may be the best to use, saving special colors and fonts for emphasis in specific areas.

Choosing Your Font

Wherever possible, use standard, very easy-to-read fonts. Many Web sites use Arial as a font, for example, because it's much easier for visitors to read than even one of the common sans serif fonts such as Times New Roman. Experiment as much as you want, but be sure that your choice is clearly readable at the size of font you choose. For most Web sites, no smaller than a 10- or 12-point size should be used for normal text. Larger points should be used for emphasis. WebSite Complete offers a short list of available fonts, including Arial, Comic Sans MS, Courier New, Impact, Times New Roman, Trebuchet MS, Verdana, and Webdings (not an alphabetical character set, but small icons suitable for use on a Web site).

Tip

If you're familiar with working in other Windows-based applications such as WordPad, Microsoft Word, or Microsoft Works, you'll find that WebSite Complete follows the same conventions for inserting, deleting, and reformatting text. You can even create your text in other applications and then copy and paste it into the appropriate area of your Web page.

Adding Text

Adding text to your site is one of the simplest tasks you can do:

1. Place your cursor where you want the text to appear.

2. Start typing your text.

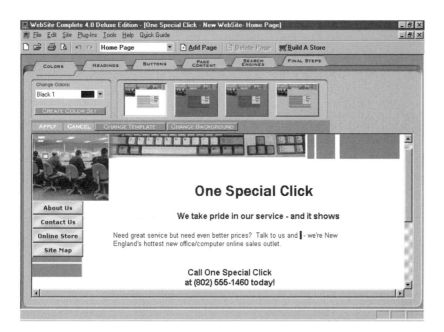

Tip

When adding many lines of text, use Shift+Enter to shorten the gap between lines.

Modifying Text

To modify existing text (including some or all of the default text placed in your project by WebSite Complete as an example), follow these steps:

1. Locate the area of text you want to modify.

2. Highlight the text.

3. Type in your replacement text.

Changing Text Color

You also have the option of changing the color of your text. Such modification can be done to one line, one paragraph, one article, or throughout the page. Follow these steps to do so:

1. Locate and highlight the desired text.

2. From the formatting toolbar that will appear above your Web site window (at the bottom of Control Panel), click the underlined letter A.

3. A window that offers a color palette will appear; double-click the preferred color for the text, as seen below.

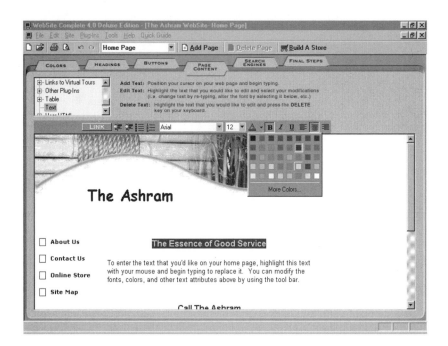

Working with Buttons

Buttons on Web pages are small images used as navigational tools. They not only help get a visitor's attention, but they also function as an underlined hyperlink. Buttons, when clicked, can be used to do the following:

◆ take the visitor to another page on this site or to another site

- run a Web application or script

- open an e-mail form, addressed to the Web site's contact person, which the visitor can fill out and send

WebSite Complete allows you to change both the image used with a button and the label appearing on the button, as well as to create a **mouseover** effect. Some change color, some shimmer, and some change into another look, for example. This effect isn't mandatory, but can make for a more professional and creative appearance and can indicate that a site is well thought-out and well packaged.

mouseover
a special effect applied to a button (or other object) on a Web page that allows the object to change appearance when a (mouse) cursor passes over it or clicks it

Adding or Modifying Buttons

To change (or add) a button, or change a button's features, follow these steps:

1. Open WebSite Complete to the page that contains buttons you want to add or modify. Select the appropriate button or area and click the Buttons tab in Control Panel.

2. Refer to the Preview button to see what button (if any) is currently selected.

3. Click the Image button.

4. From the screen of button options presented in the Select an Image screen, click the new button type you want to use.

From this screen, you may also do the following:

- Click Image Type to choose Buttons, Custom, or Images

- Click Collection to choose from buttons of various themes (if you choose other than General, you'll be prompted to insert your Web-Site Complete CD to load additional button types)

- Click the Image Lab button next to the Special Effects field to make changes to the button

- Click the Browse button next to the Use My Own field to select a button image that you have obtained on your own

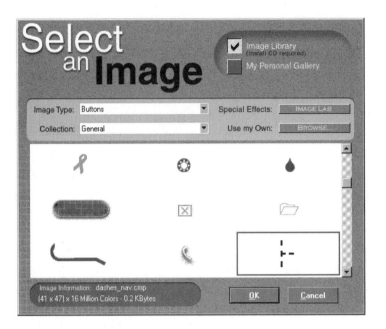

5. When prompted, choose whether you want the button to replace only the current button selected, the buttons that match the one you're currently using on all pages of your Web site, or all buttons on all pages (for a global replacement). Then click OK.

6. Check the text box to make certain that the button's text appears as desired; if not, retype it.

Enabling Mouseovers

Follow these steps to enable mouseovers for your button:

1. Open WebSite Complete to the page that contains buttons you want to add or modify. Select that button or area and click the Buttons tab in Control Panel.

2. Click to check the Enable Mouseover option (if it already has a check, leave it).

3. Go to the drop-down menu above the check box and choose Edit Mouseover (rather than the default Edit Button, as shown below).

4. Type in the text that you would like to appear when a mouse is passed over or clicks the button (such as **Click Here** or **Jump to Page**).

5. Click the Image button and follow the steps for adding a different image to your mouseover (the image that the original button changes to when a mouseover occurs).

6. When finished, click the File menu and select Preview Site (or use the Preview button on the toolbar) to view your results.

Working with Images

Take a look back at the templates that WebSite Complete supplies or at the Web you're currently building. You'll see that some graphics, referred to as images in WebSite Complete, are included by default. You may want to add more of your own, replace the existing images with ones you provide, or modify others.

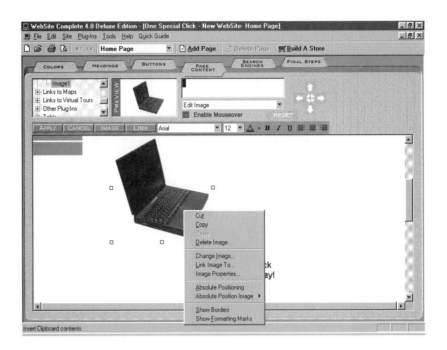

Adding an Image

To add an image to a page, follow these steps:

1. From the page in which you want to add the graphic, right-click where you want the image to appear and choose Insert Image.

2. From the resulting Select an Image window, either double-click to select one of the images listed or click Browse and provide the location of a different graphic you want to use.

3. When you've located your selection, click OK.

The image is then inserted into your Web page.

Replacing an Image

To change an image already included in a Web page, try this:

1. Locate the image you want to change.

2. Right-click the image and select Change Image.

3. From the resulting Select an Image window, either double-click to select one of the images listed or click Browse and provide the location of a different graphic you want to use.

4. When you've located your selection, click OK.

The image is immediately replaced with the new image.

Modifying Images with Image Lab

Image Lab is a WebSite Complete tool you use to apply special effects to the images on your Web site. These effects can be used one at a time or layered by selecting multiple effects for more interesting results.

Warning

Here are a few words of caution when using Image Lab. First, keep a copy of your original image, particularly if it's original artwork scanned into the computer or imported from a digital camera. This ensures that you have a fresh, original copy to work from in case you don't like the effects you apply, and it allows you to feel comfortable experimenting as much as you like. Second, exercise care in using special effects so that they don't cross the boundary from interesting to hard-to-decipher. Some images naturally lend themselves to a straightforward presentation even without effects, while others may be favorably enhanced through use. When you get into testing your site later, you can have others evaluate the effects for feedback on what works.

Follow these steps to load and use Image Lab:

1. Open the WebSite Complete site that you're building. From your Web page, or from an existing image on your Web page, right-click and choose Insert Image.

2. From the Select an Image window, select and highlight an image from either the Image Library or My Personal Gallery.

3. Click the Image Lab button to load this feature.

4. From the options window on the left of the Image Lab Special Effects screen, select an effect and click Try Effect.

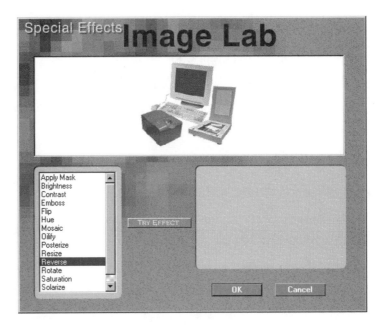

5. Modify that effect by using the settings options to the right of the effect.

6. Click the Apply Effect button.

7. Once you're satisfied with the results, click OK and then click OK again.

Modifying Images with the Right-Click Menu

From the previous procedure, you know that right-clicking an existing image produces a menu that offers options for controlling which image is placed and how it will appear.

Again, take a quick look at the menu by right-clicking an image on your site, and note these choices that are in addition to the usual ones (Cut, Copy, Delete, and Paste):

◇ Use Change Image as detailed earlier in this section.

- Use Link Image to connect an e-mail address, Web site, or other type of link to the image so that a visitor can click the image to link to that other entity.

- Use Image Properties to find out basic information about the size and type of image being used.

- Use Absolute Positioning to anchor text and image to a specific position on your page (instead of the position where automatic formatting leaves it).

- Use Absolute Positioning with Image to move an image to a specific position on your page.

- Use Show Borders to display borders used for this image on the page.

- Use Show Formatting Marks to indicate how the formatting is set for the image as it sits on this page.

You may want to try out these options to see what information or feature is available with each and how you may use them in designing your site.

Note

The Absolute Positioning feature does not work in some Web browsers. In this case, the image will appear in the upper-left corner when users view the site.

Changing Location of an Image or Text on a Page

If you don't like the location of a particular graphic or bit of text on your Web page, WebSite Complete offers you three different ways to move it.

Method #1

This is the classic cut-and-paste technique for moving objects around in a window (it works for graphics or text):

1. From your open Web site, locate the image or highlight the text you want to move and right-click on it.

2. From the resulting menu, choose Cut to remove it from its current location.

3. Move your cursor to the desired new location for the image or text.

4. Right-click and choose Paste.

The image or text you removed from its original location is now pasted into its new location.

Method #2

This is the standard drag-and-drop technique you would use in other applications:

1. From your open Web site, move your mouse cursor to the image or highlighted text you want to move.

2. Press and hold the left mouse button.

3. Drag the image or text to its newly desired location.

4. Drop the image or text into its new location by releasing the left mouse button.

The image or text you removed from its original location is now dropped into its new location.

 Warning

There are two situations in which you cannot simply relocate an image quite the way you may like. First, if you have an image with text attached or wrapped around it, this will not relocate. Also, if you insert a graphic into the middle of a field of text, the graphic will appear sandwiched between the text, without text wrapping around it.

Method #3

This technique repositions your image or text to the far left, far right, or center of your page, still within its same basic location. Use the first two methods if you want to actually move the image or text to a different part of the page. Use the latter if you want to simply reposition it uniformly in the same basic location. Follow these steps to use this method:

1. From your open Web site, move your mouse cursor to the image or highlighted text you want to reposition and then select that image.

2. Jump to the toolbar, where the alignment buttons are located.

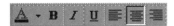

3. Choose Left, Center, or Right alignment.

The image or text is now realigned appropriately.

Working with Links

Links, or hyperlinks, establish a bridge between the current page on a Web site being viewed and a new page on the same site, a page on a different Web site, or a special program or script that can be run on the Web site. You can also create a link to bring up the visitor's e-mail window with your Web site contact's e-mail address already filled in so that customers can easily contact you if desired.

The most useful attribute of links is that they require the visitor to *do* one simple thing: click the underlined text, button, or image to which a link has been applied. Instead of entering a long, difficult Web address to connect to another page or site, for example, the user can read and click just a single word in a body of text to link. A link is, therefore, more user-friendly and more eye-friendly. Remember that eye appeal is critical in a graphical environment such as the Web.

Follow these steps to add a link to a page on your Web site:

1. From your open Web site, locate and highlight the text or image to which you want to apply a link.

2. Click the Link button at the bottom of Control Panel.

3. In the Link To window, choose the type of link you're creating and then supply the address you're linking to. For example, to link to my e-mail box, I'd type something like `mailto:kchase@kchase.com`, or to link to a page on my site, I'd type something like `http://www.kchase.com/newuser.htm`.

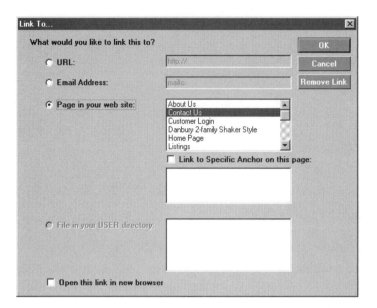

4. To have the visitor's browser open another window to display this new link rather than move the visitor from your current page, click the Open This Link in New Browser option to check it and then click OK.

> **Tip**
>
> To link a button to another Web page or e-mail, right-click the button, select Link Button To, choose the type, and provide the link address.

> **Note**
>
> In the Link To window, you'll notice the Link to Specific Anchor on This Page check box. WebSite Complete v4.0 offers the ability to add anchor links, allowing site visitors to jump from one part of a Web page to another. Go Daddy's online help takes you through the steps of this process.

Creating New Pages

You already know that Web sites, particularly professional or commercial ones, are a collection of pages published together in one site. Thus, one of the tasks you're apt to do fairly often is to add new pages to your Web site, extending the number of pages WebSite Complete sets up for you when it first builds your template.

You could create a new Web page for a variety of reasons: to tackle a new subject, to provide specialized information and more detail about a subject on another page, or to organize different products and services, for example.

Take these steps to create a new page for your Web project:

1. Open the Web to which you want to add a page and click the Add a Page option on the toolbar.

2. From the Add Web Page window, choose or provide the following:

   ◇ In Step 1: Select Page Type, click the drop-down menu and choose the page type (Standard Template, Contact Us, Event Calendar, etc.).

   ◇ In Step 2: Enter Page Heading, type the title of the Web page you're adding.

   ◇ In Step 3: Enter Button Title, type the name of this new Web page as you would like it to appear on buttons linking to this page.

   ◇ In Step 4: Select Page to Link From, click the drop-down menu to choose the title of an existing page, such as Home Page (recommended), where you would like a link to this new page to appear.

3. Click Next.

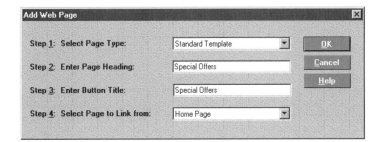

 Note

Depending on the type of page you choose, you may have an intervening screen (usually to ask configuration questions for the page) before the new page opens for your view. A good example of this is when you choose Event Calendar and you get a screen where you're asked to Add (or Delete) Events. You'll learn how to include some of these special add-ons and pages in the next chapter.

Once the new page opens on your screen, below Control Panel, you can begin adding and/or modifying text and images, as you wish. When you finish and save, it will be saved as part of the Web you're building, and will be published along with your Home page and other pages to the Web host's server.

Making Deletions

As you build your e-commerce site, it's very possible that you will, through trial and error, have images, text, or even whole pages of practice Web projects you want to delete before you finalize your Web site and prepare it to be published to an accessible Web server. The following sections cover how to make such deletions.

Deleting Text

To quickly delete simple letters or a small number of words, you can either backspace over the text or position your mouse cursor and click the Delete key.

To remove whole sentences, paragraphs, or an entire text block, you will want perform the usual block-deletion technique:

1. Position your cursor at the beginning of the text you want to delete, hold down the left button of your mouse, and drag it to the end of the desired text.

2. With the text now highlighted, release the left mouse button.

3. Right-click the highlighted area and choose Delete.

Deleting an Image

The use of many images, particularly ones that have a large file size—say an image file size of 100K versus a file size of 10K or under—may dramatically slow down the speed at which the page displays for a visitor accessing it over the Internet. While pages may draw pretty quickly on your local PC before they are published, they have to move over old telephone lines for many Internet users.

You may decide to delete an image (or multiple images) to speed up the page display, or because you don't like the image or feel it's necessary.

Follow these steps to remove an image you've placed on a Web page:

1. Click to select an image on your Web page.

2. Press the Delete key.

3. When prompted, click Yes to confirm the deletion.

Here's another way to do the very same thing:

1. Right-click an image on your Web page

2. Select Delete Image from the menu.

3. When prompted, click Yes to confirm the deletion.

Deleting a Page in Your Web

You may decide as you're working, or just before you publish your site, that you want to remove a page currently residing in your Web project.

Follow these steps to delete a page:

1. From WebSite Complete, open the page you wish to delete.

2. Click the Site option on the menu bar and choose Delete Page.

3. When prompted, confirm the deletion by clicking Yes.

Warning

If you choose to delete a page in the Web you're creating, do so thoughtfully. Once the deletion is performed in WebSite Complete, the page cannot be recovered. Check to be sure the page contains nothing you want to keep. If it does, consider moving the content to another page *before* you delete.

Deleting a Web Project from WebSite Complete

You can delete Web projects from the Welcome Back screen you receive when you reload WebSite Complete. Just follow steps 2 and 3 below. When you're already running the software on your desktop, perform all of the following steps:

1. Click the File option on the menu bar, and select New (or Open, either will work) to open the Welcome Back screen.

2. In the right panel, your existing Web projects are listed; select the one you want to delete.

Note

If you want to select a Web project to remove but the dimmed Delete button prevents you from clicking it, then you're trying to delete a Web project that you already have open in WebSite Complete. Close the Web by choosing File ➢ Close, and then try again.

3. Click the Delete button and then click Finished to return to or to open your main working screen.

Warning

Once a Web project is deleted, it's gone. So keep the Web project until you either copy out to another project any contents you want or you're certain you no longer want it.

Setting Up an Online Store on Your E-Commerce Site

While this subject is covered in much greater depth in Chapter 9, "Building Your Online Store," it's helpful now to learn about the added difficulties in selling products or services on a Web site, as well as to appreciate how much easier WebSite Complete makes the process.

By using the Build Online Store feature, WebSite Complete steps you through all the nitty-gritty details with relative ease. The software anticipates what you may need and then offers you options for setting it all up. While you originate and customize the online store on your PC as you work in the WebSite Complete software, the actual online store isn't created until you publish your e-commerce site containing that online store to Web servers that support it.

What happens on your end is that the software takes the information it gathers from you and compiles it into a database that is uploaded when your Web site is uploaded to Go Daddy–enabled Web servers. That database then becomes part of the online merchant capabilities available from these servers (such as the creation of an online Shopping Cart in which customers "drop" items they wish to purchase and the processing of credit card payments live while the customer waits for confirmation). You can think of it as your small PC hooking into a much bigger networked computer with lots more speed, security, and programs to process all the work. The server end then helps you manage your online store by providing you with special options, reports on the sale activity, and receivable accounts for your online e-store.

It may benefit you—before you move on to the next step of setting up an online store—to first master the building of your basic e-commerce site, without the online sales plugged in. This can give you more freedom to experiment before you move to the next step.

Then, once you craft a design that works in overall look, feel, and operation, and that has the introductory text and images you want, you can incorporate the online store component into your site for publishing.

Saving Your Work

One thing you may notice missing from the File menu option that you see in almost every application is a Save option. WebSite Complete automates a lot of this for you. If at any point you choose to exit from WebSite Complete, your work will be saved automatically. Also, modifications you make during a session are constantly being saved so that the files created by WebSite Complete are updated as you work.

It's still a wise idea, however, to back up a Web project on a regular basis. After all, you don't want to lose any work if there's a problem with your hard drive or some other component of your PC.

Follow these steps to make a backup of your project:

1. Click the File option and select Backup.

2. From the Backup and Restore Project window, click to select a project from the list.

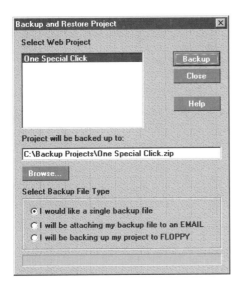

3. Below this field, note the current backup location for the backup file to be created; click the Browse button to locate and select an alternative backup location, if desired.

4. Under Select Backup File Type, choose to do one of the following options:

◇ Create a single backup file (in the location cited in step 3).

◇ Create a backup and send it as an e-mail attachment.

◇ Try to fit the Web you create onto a blank, formatted disk you have inserted into the disk drive.

5. Click the Backup button.

Chapter 5

Adding Special Features to Your E-Commerce Web Site

From the previous chapter, you know how to create a basic Web site in WebSite Complete as well as how to modify the core elements of that site by adding, deleting, or modifying templates, text, images, buttons, and links.

This chapter covers special features such as advanced customization, adding HTML code to your page, adding a calendar of events, making files or music available on your Web site, and using animation. In this chapter, you will follow along through the development of various add-ons, or plug-ins, you can use to evolve your commercial Web site from the basic template WebSite Complete has provided you.

Exploring Add-On Options

What are some uses for these add-ons?

- ◇ Real estate sites could offer more than just listings of the properties they're trying to lease or sell for clients. They could also feature links to map services that help visitors determine the overall location of the property presented in a home listing as well as a loan calculator for determining how much the interest payments on the mortgage of a chosen property may cost.

- ◇ An e-commerce site selling music might provide a bit of a song to be played as a background sound when a visitor first enters the Web site, or make audio files—perhaps samples of the music (within copyright restrictions)—available for visitors to play before buying.

- ◇ A commercial site selling computers and software may choose to make downloadable files available (patches, fixes, drivers, and utilities, for example) to customers buying their products. Online specials may be emphasized through the use of a scrolling marquee (available as a **plug-in** from WebSite Complete) that slides across the main Web screen the way that an announcement crawls across the screen during a TV program.

Obviously, many of the extra features that can be added to a commercial site are available by building an online store, which you already know you can do with WebSite Complete. However, details on building and managing facets of an online store will be covered in detail in Chapter 9, "Building Your Online Store."

Adding Your Own HTML

HTML allows you to achieve a specific function or design option and is freely available all over the Internet. Many Web sites are devoted to showing budding Web masters how to do fancy tricks such as setting up special tables, creating interesting boxes, or developing an interactive user function such as a user survey.

While WebSite Complete removes the necessity of learning HTML to produce a professional-looking Web site, it also supports the inclusion of HTML code in a Web site. Therefore, if you find a trick you want to try, you can plug the HTML code in and let it run as part of your Web site.

plug-in
a tool that can be plugged into and used from a Web page

One example of a situation where you may need to add HTML code is if you sign up with a Web site promotion program such as Link Exchange. To be a member and be promoted by them, you must agree to carry a banner ad for the service on your Web site. To enable you to run this banner ad, they supply you with HTML code to add to your home page.

Warning

Using HTML in a WebSite Complete site removes some of your Go Daddy support.

You add HTML code through WebSite Complete by using the HTML Editor provided in the software. Follow these steps to load and use the editor to add code:

1. With WebSite Complete open to the desired page in your Web, click the Page Content tab in Control Panel.

2. From the Page Content screen, look in the treeview panel in the upper-left corner of Control Panel and select User HTML.

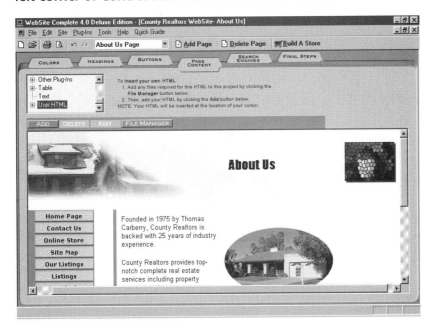

3. Click Add.

4. Type in an identifying name for the HTML code you are adding; make it a name that will help you recall this code later, if needed.

5. In the large text field in HTML Editor, as seen below, type or paste in the HTML code you want to add.

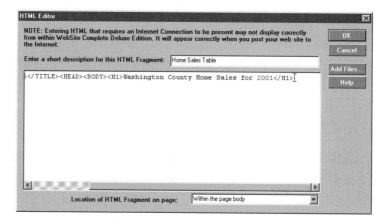

6. Click the Add Files button *if* you know that the HTML code you're adding requires extra files to support it, such as external programs or other files, images, or sound files, and then choose the necessary files.

7. Click the drop-down menu in the lower-right half of HTML Editor, select the location of the current page in which this HTML code should be placed (if in doubt, pick a relatively empty area of the page), and then click OK.

If you later want to change the location of the HTML code on this Web page (or even move it to another page), you can simply drag and drop it to a new area.

Adding and Editing Tables

New to WebSite Complete v4.0 is the ability to add tables to your Web pages. Tables can be used on a Web site much as you would use them in a normal document: to help organize information easily and at a glance.

Follow these steps to create a new Web page for your site and add a table to it:

1. With WebSite Complete open to your Web project, click the Add a Page option on the toolbar.

2. From the Add Web Page window, select the page type, provide a page heading and button title for this new page, and select a page (such as Home Page) on which to provide a link for this new page.

3. In the new page, click the portion of the page where you want the table to appear.

4. In the treeview panel, click Table and then click the New option below it, which will display a table format on your Web page.

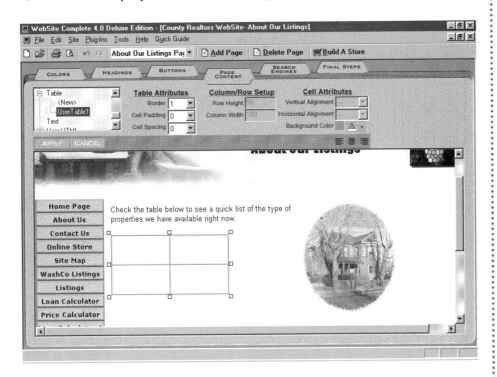

5. Click in one of the boxes in the table outline to begin adding text (including statistics and numbers) or images to your table.

6. In the Control Panel part of the page, use these adjustment options: Table Attributes (with the additional Border, Cell Padding, or Cell Spacing options), Column/Row Setup, and Cell Attributes.

If you need to delete a table you've added, you can do so by following these steps:

1. With WebSite Complete open to the Web page on which you want to remove the table, right-click on a cell within the table.

2. From the menu, click Table Commands.

3. From the submenu, choose Delete Table.

4. When prompted to confirm your choice to delete, click Yes.

Adding or Deleting Rows

If you want to add rows to or delete rows from a table, follow these steps:

1. Right-click in a cell within the table to which you want to add (or from which you want to delete) a row.

2. From the menu, choose the Table Commands option.

3. From the submenu, choose either Insert Row or Delete Row, as appropriate.

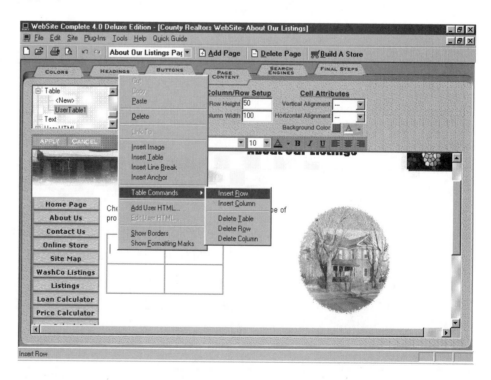

Adding or Deleting Columns

If you need to add columns to or delete columns from a table, perform these steps:

1. Right-click in a cell within the table to which you want to add (or from which you want to delete) a column.

2. From the menu, choose the Table Commands option.

3. From the submenu, choose either Insert Column or Delete Column, as appropriate.

Adding Special Files

Different types of files may be added to your site to either enhance the overall ambience of the site or to support users. It's how you add these files to your site that determines how visitors will experience them—a sound file that plays automatically for them versus one they must click or download to play.

Adding Sound Files

There are two major ways you can provide audio, or sound, files to your Web site. One way sets up a sound file that plays whenever a visitor first enters your Web site. This is called a background sound, because the music plays in the background while the visitor browses the site.

The second type involves creating a sound file in a format that can be downloaded and listened to by visitors through an installed audio application such as Microsoft Windows Media Player™ or RealNetworks® RealPlayer® (both are online media player applications). All they have to do is click the link to this sound file to initiate the process. As you may recall, RealPlayer and RealProducer® were two of the bonus software packages available on the WebSite Complete CD you installed in Chapter 2, "Getting Started with WebSite Complete 4.0."

Adding Background Sound

Background sound differs from other types of sound files you normally place on a Web site in that it requires no user intervention (a click by a Web site visitor) to initiate. Unless the visitor doesn't have a sound card installed or has disabled the sound option in his or her browser software, just opening your Web site will load and play the background sound you placed there. Unless the visitor presses the Stop button on their browser's toolbar, the background sound will continue to play for however long you've designated it to do so.

For this reason, you should use background sound judiciously. After all, your intent isn't to annoy, but to enhance the visitor's experience. To paraphrase the old saying: One person's favorite song is another person's worst nightmare. While more savvy visitors will know how to stop an annoying sound file from playing automatically, many won't. They may think the only way to stop that "awful" sound is to leave your Web site or close their Web browser. If they do that, it's a potential sale or customer you have lost.

Also, whenever you work with sound files, be careful that you are not violating any copyright or usage laws by using someone else's work (part of a song, a recording from a TV or radio program, or a recording of someone speaking). Some require prior written permission to use them, charge a royalty fee, or may exclude any commercial use of them (and an e-commerce site is a commercial entity).

Tip

If you're new to the concept of digital sound and sound files, understand that recordings made off the computer (an audio recording of a radio program, for example) have to be converted into a special digital format to be understood by your PC. You can, however, record directly onto the PC by using a microphone connected to your PC's sound card connection at the back of the PC, through a cable connection between your CD drive and your sound card, through a TV card installed on your PC, and by other methods.

Once you have a sound file you want to use for a background file, there are only a few steps necessary to include the sound on your site:

1. With WebSite Complete, open your Home page.

2. Click the Page Content tab in Control Panel.

3. Locate and highlight the Background Sound listing in this tab's treeview (upper-left corner of Control Panel), as shown on the next page.

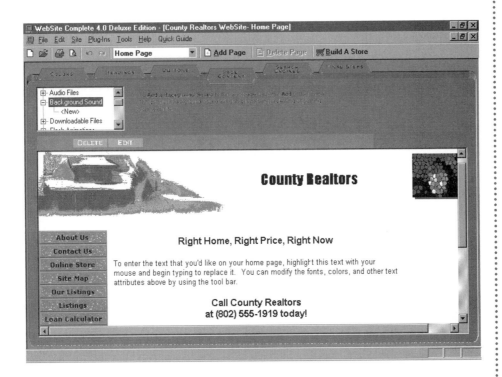

4. Click Add.

5. When prompted, select the location of the sound file you want to use, highlight the sound file, and click Open.

When complete, your sound file is installed to play in the background when a visitor arrives on your Web site.

Adding Other Sound Files

You can add sound files that do allow visitors to choose whether to play them or not. Instead of starting automatically, as with background sounds, the visitor must click a link—and this link can be text, an image, a button, or an icon—to the sound file in order to play it.

These are the steps necessary to add this type of sound file:

1. With WebSite Complete open to the page on which you want to add a sound file, click the Page Content tab in Control Panel.

2. Highlight the Audio Files option in the treeview at the upper-left corner of Control Panel.

3. Click Add.

4. Locate and select the sound file you want to use, and then click Open.

This method now displays a link to your chosen sound file in the form of an audio icon that visitors may click.

Adding Files for Downloading

Many different types of e-commerce sites make files available for their visitors and customers to download. The file in question could be a monthly newsletter in text format, a catalog, or an online product manual.

Warning

Any files uploaded to a Web site should be checked for computer viruses before being made available to the public for download (although it's difficult to infect sound and graphics files). If you want to offer files, get a virus-scanning program to use. Make sure to check your documentation for instructions on keeping your antivirus program updated to protect against recently detected viruses.

Follow these steps to make a file available for download from a page on your Web site:

1. From WebSite Complete, open to the page on which you want to add the downloadable file and click the Page Content tab in Control Panel.

2. In the treeview window, locate and highlight Downloadable Files.

3. Click Add.

4. Locate and select the file you want to make available and click Open.

Note

Looking for sound files to use? WebSite Complete automatically installs a few collections of sounds when you set it up. You'll find them in the Go Daddy folder on your hard drive, with these subfolder names: Background Sounds, Human Sounds and Phrases, Miscellaneous, and Musical Instruments.

When you're done, a Download File icon will appear on your Web page. Visitors can click this icon to start downloading the file.

Flash Animation and WebSite Complete

Many Web sites today—especially the upscale, professionally polished ones—use **Flash Animation** entry screens to give visitors a splash of color and movement as they enter their sites. Flash Animation usually involves the use of symbols or shapes (or their components) moving across the screen in an evolving pattern.

Other, smaller animations inserted like an image into an existing Web page (rather than as a separate page) can serve to grab a visitor's attention and cause some to explore your site further and see what else you have. Depending on the type of animation chosen, the mood it sets can be dramatic, fun and whimsical, thoughtful, or technically dazzling.

Adding a Customized Flash Animation Entry to Your Site

Entry screen animations are normally the first screen a visitor sees when accessing your Web site. Such animations lend themselves to having a page of their own and including a clickable link to your main site, because this type of Flash animation tends to be larger. And you already know that the larger the graphic (and this is a special graphic that moves), the slower the page loads. So you want the visitor to see it perhaps only once and then move beyond it into the regular site where the page will load more quickly.

WebSite Complete makes it possible for you to obtain—and customize—such an entry screen for your site at no cost and with very little work on your part. You

Flash Animation

a hot graphics applet, owned by a company named Macromedia, that can add a splashy and sometimes dramatic look to Web sites by using eye-catching, fast-loading, moving Web page graphics as an entry screen or as a special in-page image

99

initiate this feature by clicking the Plug-Ins option on the menu bar and selecting Flash Entry Page.

If you're not already connected to the Internet when you attempt to use this feature, you'll be prompted to click a button to connect. Even after clicking this button, you may still see it again. Just click it until the software recognizes your connection.

You're then presented with a page full of Web clip samples made available for customization to WebSite Complete owners. Choose one by clicking the Customize This Clip button, or use the arrows at the bottom of the page to check through other options.

Flash Generator

a helpful wizard that helps you select, modify, and generate a Flash animation for your Web site

Once you select one, a **Flash Generator** screen will appear. At the top left of the screen, you'll see an Editable Objects menu. Choose any of the following to customize your Flash animation:

❖ Background to modify the current background of the animation

❖ Text 1 to type in the text you want to appear here (can be company name, a special message, etc.)

❖ Text 2 (same as Text 1)

❖ Text 3 (same as Text 2)

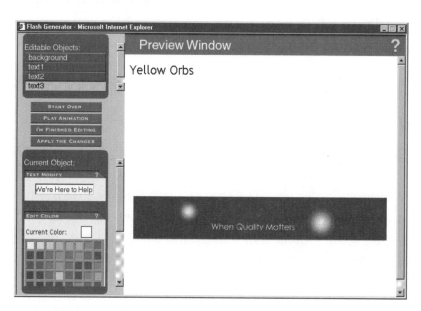

Below Editable Objects, you'll see four buttons indicating your options. These include the following:

- ◆ Start Over to scrap the current animation and start fresh

- ◆ Play Animation to show the animation as it will appear to Web site visitors

- ◆ I'm Finished Editing to click when you finish making changes and are satisfied with your results

- ◆ Apply the Changes to click when you're ready to save your animation changes

You'll then see a Shopping Cart appear—you're now connected to an e-commerce site, after all—and you can review your Flash Clip animation order. The normal price for this animation is $19.95, but your cost will be $0 because of the special promotion available to you as a new WebSite Complete user.

Review the order and click the Continue with Checkout button. You'll be prompted to supply your name and shipping information to receive your CD containing the customized animation. Fill in the info and click Continue with Checkout. Finally, click Complete Your Purchase to finish placing your order. You'll then be given order details you can print and save. When you click Close to shut the order screen, WebSite Complete will automatically switch itself to the Page Content tab in Control Panel, reconnect with Go Daddy's gateway to the Internet, and retrieve the Flash Clip you just customized.

What you should also note is that Flash Animation now appears as an option in the treeview at the upper-left corner of Control Panel. Below this, click the Add button to add this animation clip to your page. This new page of **Flash Intros**, titled whatever you assigned to the Text 1 entry, is added to the collection of pages making up your Web site, and will be available as an entry into your site when you publish it.

Flash Intros
full-screen moving graphics leading into your Web site's home page

Adding a Flash Animation to Another Page

Besides Flash entry screens, you can add a Flash animation to other pages on your Web site. For this, you're adding the animation to another page rather than making the animation into a freestanding page. Naturally, you should add animations that are smaller than those used in the full-screen pages.

Follow these steps to accomplish this:

1. With WebSite Complete loaded and open to the page in which you want to add a Flash animation, click the Page Content tab in Control Panel.

2. From the treeview window at the upper-left corner of the Page Content screen, locate and click Flash Animation; then choose New.

3. If you're not already connected to the Internet, a button will prompt you to connect (or you'll receive instructions for doing it manually).

4. Once logged on to the support site, you'll receive a screen asking you to pick one of the clip categories. Click to choose Flash Animation: Clips for Any Page.

5. To use an animation you like from the free choices, click Customize This Clip.

6. Edit the background and text fields, apply your changes, and go through the ordering screen. Then add the animation, as detailed in the previous section on Flash Animation entry screens.

Adding an Event Calendar

Many commercial sites post an event calendar, much as merchants might post a calendar or listing of store events in a physical store. For example, a video retailer setting up shop on the Web might use a calendar of events to announce the dates of new video releases or when special promotions occur. A physical store developing an online presence could use the calendar of events to announce various in-store sales, demonstrations, or classes.

Here's an example of online promotion success as demonstrated by a local gourmet-cooking store that has an attached cooking school: The store/school location is off the beaten path, but their Web presence and calendar of events have helped in bringing a whole new audience of shoppers and cooking students from an 80-mile radius to their building.

Note

To use the Event Calendar feature, you must use Go Daddy to host your Web site.

Creating Your Event Calendar

There are two different ways you can launch the process of creating an event calendar for your site, as you'll see in step 1:

1. From WebSite Complete, click the Plug-Ins option on the menu bar and click Event Calendar.

Or, click Add Page on the toolbar and choose Events Page from the list of page options; the software opens an Events Page and loads the Event Calendar Manager, as shown below:

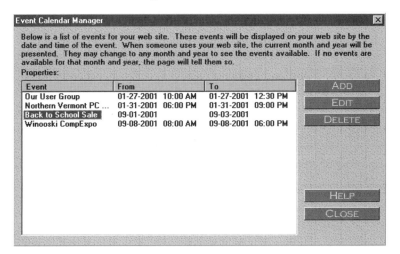

2. Click Add.

3. From the Add Event window, type or select the information about the first event you want to add (events are added one at a time).

4. Click Apply to save this event to your calendar, or click Edit to correct an error in the event you added. Then click Apply.

5. Repeat, as needed, to add more events to the calendar.

6. When finished, click Close; your event calendar is now complete.

7. Click the File option on the menu and select Preview Web (or click Preview from the toolbar) to view your newly created event calendar.

Note

Your event calendar will look slightly different to your Web site visitors than to you as you view it on your system before you publish it. Thus, you should be sure to check this page after you publish your site to be sure it looks exactly the way you want it to appear.

Once your site is published, visitors will be able to click the link to your event calendar and see a display of the current month's events. If there are no events scheduled for the current month, a message saying so will display. However, visitors can click the drop-down menu to choose another month to check for events.

Editing the Events

After you've created your event calendar, you can still go back to modify entries as you deem necessary:

1. Click the Plug-Ins option on the menu bar and select Event Calendar.

2. Select a listed event to modify, and click Edit.

3. Make your modification(s).

4. Click Close.

When you close the manager, your calendar is automatically updated with the new information. However, if it's already been published to your Web host, you will need to republish so that the update is seen by visitors. You'll learn how to publish in the next chapter.

Removing an Event

You may want to go in and remove old events whose dates have passed or because you no longer want to promote an event for whatever reason.

Follow these steps to remove an event using Event Calendar Manager:

1. Click the Plug-Ins option on the menu bar and select Event Calendar.

2. Select a listed event to remove, and click Delete.

3. Repeat, as necessary, until there are no further events you want to remove.

4. Click Close.

Again, you will need to republish your Web site for the calendar event deletions to be reflected on your live Web site.

Tip

Don't post an event calendar unless you plan to populate it with events. Too many commercial sites offering them either post them with no information or the information is long out-of-date. An event calendar is a nice addition to a site *only if* it's maintained regularly and shows some activity as new dates are posted; a blank or out-of-date one can make a bad impression.

Adding Options for Real Estate Web Sites

If you want to establish a Web presence to promote your property listings to a more global audience, WebSite Complete offers many of the detailed options involved in setting up the typical features of online real estate sites. These include loan and property calculators, uniform listing formats, and an option to help you link to map services to provide visitors with a geographical locator reference. Such features are handled through the use the Real Estate Listings Manager tool, available as an option on the Plug-Ins menu from the menu bar.

Setting Up Real Estate Listings

A word of advice that you likely already know but that bears restating before you begin: The more complete you make each property listing, the more likely you are to generate responses from interested parties. Informal surveys indicate that real estate shoppers tend to ignore listings containing very limited information and move instead to properties with good pictorial representation and a detailed fact sheet. With a more thorough listing, they tend to feel more inclined to contact the listing agent for more information or to schedule a showing–or dismiss it from their list of possibilities without taking your time.

> ### Note
>
> Having just purchased a new home I fell in love with based on a very complete online listing— and the site's easy ability to get me in touch with the listing agent—I think the survey results are right. Considering the increasing competition for online home shoppers, using online listings will improve your odds at selling (or leasing) a property—plus it's an inexpensive advertising tool.

Creating the First Listing

Perform these steps to create your first online real estate listing:

1. From WebSite Complete, click the Add Page option on the toolbar to create a new page in which the listings will reside.

2. Click the Plug-Ins option on the menu bar and choose Real Estate Listings Manager.

3. When the Real Estate Listings page opens, click Add.

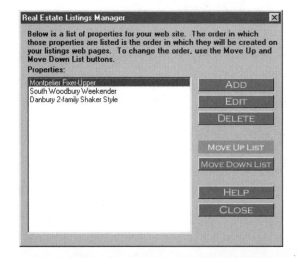

4. In the Property Listing Editor screen, make any changes to the default font type and font size (shown above) and then fill in the blank listing fields:

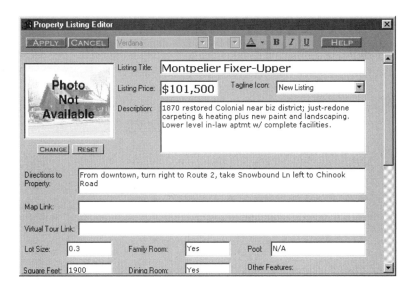

- ◇ Listing Title to give a unique identifying name for the listing

- ◇ Listing Price to type a dollar sign (**$**) followed by the property price

- ◇ Tagline Icon to choose from one of the special icons to categorize the property, including Custom Built, Just Reduced, New Listing, Must Sell, and Sale Pending

- ◇ Description to provide as complete a description as possible

- ◇ Directions to Property to give either exact directions or a general area (the latter is better if you don't want people to show up without an appointment)

- ◇ Map Link to provide a link to the map locating this property, if available

- ◇ Virtual Tour Link to provide a link to the virtual tour you've arranged to be created for this listing, if available

- ◇ Lot Size to give the size, usually in acres

- ◇ Family Room (Yes or No)

- ◇ Pool (Yes or No)

- ◇ Square Feet to give the building's size, in square feet

     ◆ Dining Room to give the size, or use N/A for not available

     ◆ Years Built to give the number of years since the building was constructed

     ◆ Kitchen to provide information about the kitchen (can provide the dimensions or a label, like "Remodeled")

     ◆ Other Features to list information about the property

5. Return to the top left of the Property Listing Editor screen and add a picture to this listing, if available, by clicking the Change button.

6. You'll be prompted to insert the CD containing the image collection; click Cancel, which loads instead the Select an Image window.

7. From Select an Image, click Browse and locate and specify the image file you want to use for this listing. You can add additional images for this listing, if you have them, in the image placeholders at the bottom of the editor.

8. When done, click Apply to save the listing.

Editing a Listing

If you need to return to and modify a listing you've published—because the status or sale price has changed, or you want to add information to what's already there—you can do so by going back to the Real Estate Listings Manager.

Then follow these steps:

1. Click the Plug-Ins option on the menu bar and select Real Estate Listings.

2. In this screen, locate and select the listing you want to modify, and then click Edit.

3. Make the necessary changes and click Apply.

The change(s) will take effect immediately on your local system, but changes to the published Web site itself won't be modified until you republish the site.

Removing a Listing

You can easily remove a listing—because it has been sold or you no longer represent the property, for example.

To remove a listing, follow these steps:

1. Click the Plug-Ins option on the menu bar and select Real Estate Listings.

2. In this screen, locate and select the listing you want to modify, and then click Delete.

As with the modifications before it, deletions won't be reflected on your online Web site until you republish, which effectively uploads the changes you made.

 Warning

Be aware that you won't receive a confirmation window when you remove a listing, so you won't get a chance to back out of the deletion if you change your mind. Thus, be sure you want to remove the listing before you do this.

Changing Listing Order

In other situations, you may have a need to rearrange the order of the listings you publish—to better feature a specific property or to change those with sales pending to the bottom of the list, for example. Here's how to do this:

1. Click the Plug-Ins option on the menu bar and select Real Estate Listings.

2. In this screen, locate and select the listing you want to relocate and click either Move Up List or Move Down List.

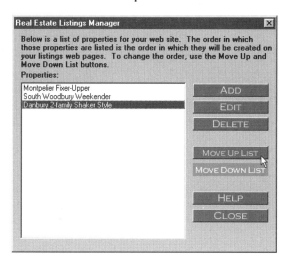

3. Repeat as necessary until the listing appears in the order you desire, and then click Close.

map link

a special type of Web hyperlink that connects a reference on a text page, such as a real estate listing, to an online map of that area

Adding a Map Link

If you have access to a good, reliable online source for mapping services to help visitors zero in on the location of a property you have listed, you can use the real estate options in WebSite Complete to point directly to the specific map. When you establish a link between a reference on a Web page and an actual map, this is called a **map link**.

Note

Probably the best known example of an online mapping service is MapQuest at www .mapquest.com. Visit this or another mapping site to see if it is a good possibility for you. Then check the service about pricing and availability.

If you establish such a service, you can add a map link to a property listing by following these steps:

1. Click the Plug-Ins option on the WebSite Complete menu bar and choose Real Estate Listings.

2. From Real Estate Listings Manager, select the listing to which you want to add a map link and click Edit to bring up the Property Listing Editor.

3. In the Map Link field, type in the URL for the map link to this property.

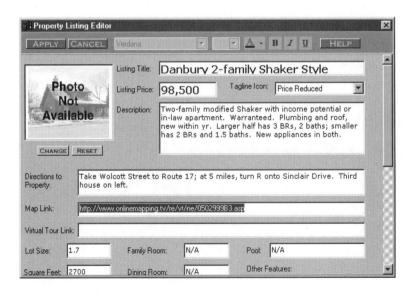

4. When finished, click Apply.

Setting Up Real Estate Calculators

Many of today's real estate listing sites offer special tools to help potential buyers determine whether they can afford the cost of the monthly payments, how much the down payment will be, and more. WebSite Complete helps you add these features—each one on its own new page as part of your site—quickly and easily.

Adding a Loan Payment Calculator

A Loan Payment Calculator helps prospective real estate shoppers gauge how much monthly mortgage payments will cost them based on a specific property. Follow these steps to add one to your site:

1. Click the Plug-Ins option on the menu bar and select Loan Payment Calculator.

2. From the Add Web Page window, verify the information presented for each. Select Page Type should show the Loan Payment Calculator; edit as needed under Enter Page Heading and Enter Button Title, and be sure that Home Page—unless you want to change it—is selected under Select Page to Link From.

3. Then click OK.

Your Loan Payment Calculator is then added automatically on its own Web page and linked to the Home page by default, as shown below.

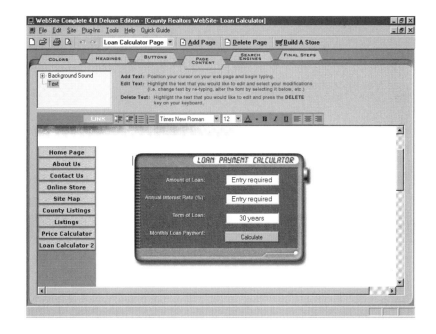

Adding a Property Price Calculator

A Property Price Calculator helps prospective buyers determine how much a property will actually cost them when the actual property price, predicted mortgage interest rate, and mortgage loan term are factored in.

To add a Property Price Calculator to your site, perform these steps:

1. Click the Plug-Ins option on the menu bar and select Property Price Calculator.

2. Confirm that the information is correct in the Add New Page window, and then click OK.

Your Property Price Calculator is then added automatically on its own Web page, linked to the Home page by default.

Adding Other Plug-Ins

There are some fairly typical Web site plug-in devices that you may want to include that don't fall into other categories such as Flash animations, event calendars, or real estate–specific functions.

You can add one of the possible plug-ins by following these steps:

1. While connected to the Internet (this is necessary to use this feature; if you're not connected, WebSite Complete will prompt to connect), open the page on which you want to add this feature, click the Plug-Ins option on the menu bar, and select Other Plug-Ins.

2. Read the Online Plug-Ins Wizard information window, and then click to close.

3. From the Plug-In screen, choose from these available plug-ins:

   ◊ Date/Time Stamp lets you put a time and date stamp on all pages you create or entries you edit.

   ◊ Hit Counter lets you count visitors to your site or to a particular page on the site; you can choose from a series of styles.

◆ Scrolling Marquee creates a dramatic, moving announcement screen. You set options for vertical or horizontal presentation, font type and color, speed of the presentation, size of the marquee, and the displayed message.

As with Flash Animation, you'll be prompted to provide ordering information. There is no fee for obtaining and including these plug-ins on your Web site.

Warning

When you view your Web page on your local system, you won't see the same types of plug-ins you can add here (like Hit Counter). Because these add-ons are available only when run off a host Web server, all you will see of them on your local system is a placeholder for the plug-in you've inserted. Always be sure to check these plug-ins when you review the site after you've published it.

Chapter 6
Publishing Your E-Commerce Web Site

You've now reached the point where you're almost ready to actually publish your Web site. Just a very few steps separate you from having a complete, ready-for-Web-time e-commerce site.

Right now, your Web site exists only on the hard disk of your computer, available to no one but you and whoever else may be looking over your shoulder as you work. Making the site available to the global Internet requires the actual uploading or transferring of the Web pages you created to a Web server run by a qualified Web host provider. This process is called posting.

Web publishing
the process by which the files you create as you make your Web site are transferred to a Web server, subsequently making your e-commerce site accessible to others

Before Posting Your Site

Before you take that momentous step of posting or, more commonly, **Web publishing**, you must address certain details to make sure your e-commerce site is truly ready for other eyes to view. Specifically, you need to cover the following bases:

- ✧ Review your total Web site to make sure it has everything you wanted to include the first time it's published.

- ✧ Check over the site for spelling, grammar, and display.

- ✧ Add some special searchable phrases to your site to help when someone performs a Web search.

- ✧ Establish a hosting account with a Web service provider (aka a Web host).

It's important to consider that it can take from 24–48 hours for a registered domain to become available for use. Depending on where you set up your hosting account, there also may be a delay of a day or two (possibly longer over a weekend or holiday) before you can use and publish to your newly established Web site. It's therefore wise to do this in advance if you're in a rush to get the site established. Use the time to review your Web project again and make any additional modifications.

Reviewing Your Site for Completeness

Before proceeding, take a look back at the checklist you made when planning your site in Chapter 3, "Planning Your First E-Commerce Site." Then open your site again in WebSite Complete and compare your "must have" features in your list against the site you created as you moved through Chapter 4, "Building Your First E-Commerce Web Site," and Chapter 5, "Adding Special Features to Your E-Commerce Web Site."

As you do this, ask yourself these questions:

- ✧ Did I include everything I need to have in this first publishing?

- ✧ Did I replace all the default text and images in WebSite Complete with my own?

- ◆ Have I made it easy for potential customers visiting my site to get a clear understanding of the products/services I present and how they can obtain them?

- ◆ Have I given visitors the necessary information for contacting me?

Are You Ready?

There is at least one other question to ask yourself, of course: Are *you* ready to begin your e-commerce business? You may have an initial rush of customers, especially after you take the steps outlined in Chapter 10, "Promoting Your E-Commerce Web Site," to promote your online business, although there are no guarantees. You have to be prepared to respond to all customers on a timely basis and provide them with good service, whether you become very busy or not. When people buy online, they tend to expect fast delivery of the product—a matter of days rather than a matter of weeks. If you have a product that needs to be shipped to the customer, be sure that you have the means to handle the extra workload and that you know how to pack your product so that it won't be damaged in transit. You should consider all of this before you publish your site and certainly before you begin to actively promote it.

Adding Search Words

Have you wondered what criteria are used when you use one of the major Web search engines—AltaVista®, Google©, and Yahoo!© among them—to find sites focused on a particular topic?

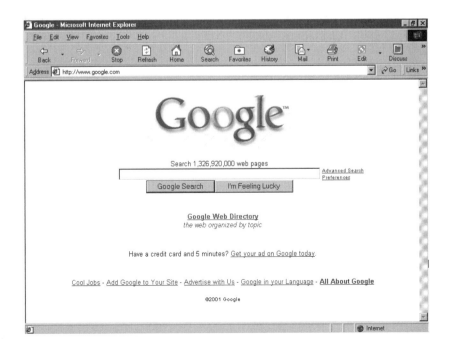

For one, major search engines do this themselves by scanning the Internet for various Web sites and taking the information they glean from those scans to supply you with search results. They organize and categorize the information by key phrases that help identify each site.

search words
words that help identify and categorize a Web site on Internet search engines

Here's an example: John Smith owns a bookstore specializing in historical texts and creates an e-commerce site to sell his books to a wider audience. John's site gets picked up by the Web search engines, and John helps this along by using **search words**. Then one day you use your Web browser to visit Yahoo! at www.yahoo.com, and you perform a search using the key phrase "battle history books." And up pops John's Web site in your search results list—along with his competition. That's how it can work for you with your e-commerce site.

A smart Web site creator supplies, as part of the background information stored on the site, certain key search words that help identify and categorize the site. This step is even more critical for an e-commerce Web owner like yourself who wants to draw in potential customers.

Follow these steps to add search words to your Web site:

1. Open WebSite Complete to your current project.

2. From Control Panel, click the Search Engines tab.

3. At the six boxes on the left (in the Search Engine Keywords field), type in searchable keywords that apply to your site. You are not limited to just six keywords; you can type multiple keywords in each box, separating each keyword with a comma.

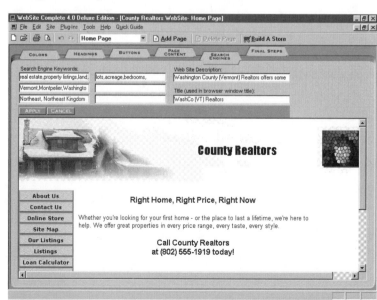

4. In the Web Site Description box on the right, provide an identifying statement about the type of site you've created. For example: "This site specializes in connecting visitors with attorneys and legal services in the greater Pacific Northwest, including affordably priced packages for real estate closings, simple wills, and uncontested divorces."

5. When complete, simply click another Control Panel tab for a prompt to save your changes.

You can return at any time to add additional search words using the steps outlined above, and then republish your Web project to your online site.

Using Meta Tags

You can find out which searchable keywords other sites like yours use by visiting the site using a browser such as Microsoft Internet Explorer (click the View menu and choose Source). You will then see the source HTML code that built this Web page, including any **meta tags** used for identifying the site in search engines.

You may have run across the term meta tags in connection with performing searches from major Web search engines such as Yahoo! or AltaVista. Meta tags are the HTML equivalent of the search words you establish. The major difference is that you don't have to learn HTML or anything else to do it. Additionally, if you're inclined to add meta tags to your site later using the HTML Editor in WebSite Complete, Go Daddy Software advises that they do not support their use.

meta tags
the HTML equivalent of
search words

Proofing Your E-Commerce Site

One common mistake made by new—and sometimes not so new—Web site creators is that they get so involved in planning and designing the site that they don't check it for problems or errors before they post it to their Web service. While you'll want to go back and check your e-commerce site again after it's posted to make certain everything works, you should also check your site before it goes live for any embarrassing typos, glaring grammatical errors, incorrect or missing information, omitted pages, or broken links.

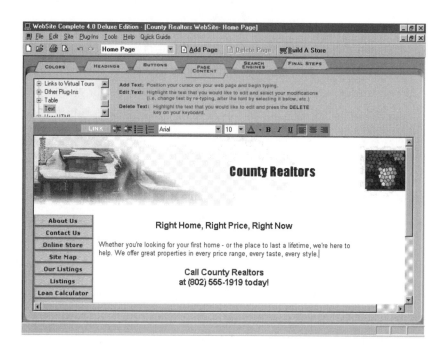

You should carefully check the following items:

- ❖ Review spelling and grammar.

- ❖ Double-check any statements or claims you make (a business or professional person can be held to a higher degree of accuracy than a layperson).

- ❖ Review images to be certain they are the ones you want to include and that no image placeholders are left (they'll show up as a blank space with a little icon on visitors' browsers if published this way).

- ❖ Verify links you've used to be sure they point to the right page or alternate Web site.

- ❖ Delete any pages you don't want to include, and make certain all the pages you wanted to include are present in your project.

- ❖ Check performance (how fast and effectively each page will load when viewed through a visitor's browser at an average connection speed).

As you already know from Chapter 5, some of the plug-ins or additional options you use, such as a scrolling marquee or a hit counter, will only work when published. Thus, you'll need to check these live on the Web after you've published to be sure they work and appear as you intended.

Performing a Review

To verify that everything is as you want it to be, you need to open your project again. There are some tools in WebSite Complete to help you check your site before publishing, but one of the best tools you'll have is your own pair of eyes. Read carefully as you review your site, with a mind toward how visitors may read it. Where possible, have a friend, family member, or colleague look at your work, too. They may spot a problem you miss because you've been so involved in creating the site.

Previewing the Site

You need to have an idea of how your published e-commerce project will look *before* you make it live by posting it to your Web server. To do this, you'll use the Preview feature in WebSite Complete:

1. With your nearly completed Web project open, click the File menu and choose Preview Site.

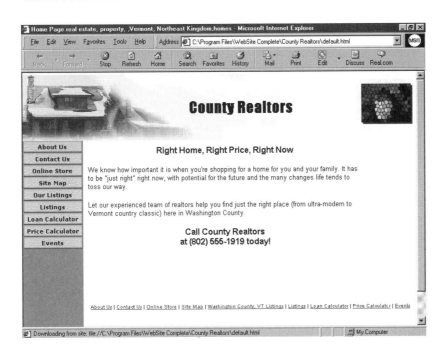

2. A warning window will alert you that all components may not be available for preview until the site is published. Click Close.

3. When your project loads in Internet Explorer, review your pages for any problems and verify the links you have set up. If all looks well, you may proceed to the next step.

Checking Your Spelling

One far too common, yet very avoidable, error that Web site creators make is the failure to spell-check a Web page. Typos and misspellings may affect how the content you provide on your e-commerce site is perceived. These errors can make it look less than professional. Not everyone who views your site will be a good speller, but they can usually spot when something is spelled incorrectly, even if they can't identify the correct spelling.

To check for spelling errors on your site, follow these steps:

1. Launch WebSite Complete and open your project.

2. Click the Final Steps tab in Control Panel.

3. Click the Spell Checker button under the Verify Web Site section on the left.

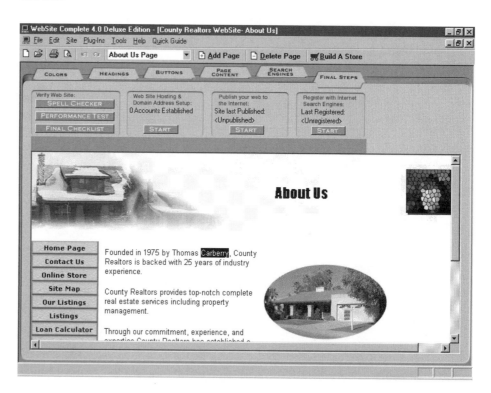

4. The spell checker will commence and then pause when it finds a word that it cannot locate in its dictionary. You then have the following options:

◇ Ignore to overlook this spelling this one time

◇ Ignore All to overlook all occurrences of this spelling (helpful for a word that you know is spelled correctly but is not in the dictionary)

◇ Change to check the Change To or Suggestions choice at the left of the Spelling window (make sure to select the correct spelling before clicking Change)

◇ Change All to do the same as above, but correcting all occurrences of this word

◇ Add to add a word to the dictionary so that it won't come up on future spell checks (make sure to verify the spelling first)

◇ Suggest to prompt the dictionary to offer known spellings of the word

◇ Options to choose from Always Suggest, Ignore Words in Uppercase, or Ignore Words with Numbers (click to check or uncheck, as desired)

◇ Close to exit the spell checker

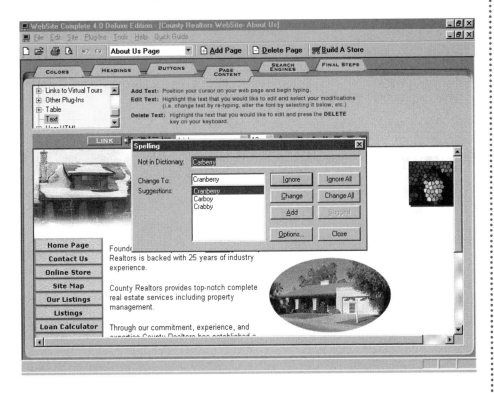

Checking Your Grammar

There is no grammar-checking tool built into WebSite Complete. One option, besides simply reviewing on your own, is to copy a block of text you want to check and paste it into a blank document in another program, such as a word processor like Microsoft Word, that does have this capability. Note any problems found in the grammar check, and make the necessary changes to your text in WebSite Complete.

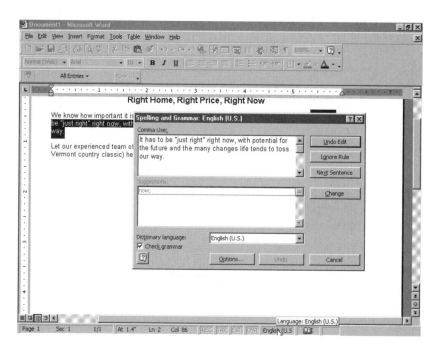

Testing Your Performance

This option allows you to get an advance look at which pages on your Web site may load too slowly for visitors—a factor that may discourage them from checking out all the products and services on your site or from making a purchase.

To check your site before you publish, follow these steps:

1. Launch WebSite Complete and open your project.

2. Click the Final Steps tab in Control Panel.

3. Click the Performance Test button under the Verify Web Site section on the left.

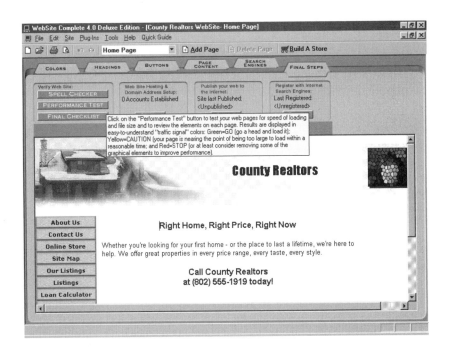

4. From the Performance Results screen, review the list of the pages included in your Web project, the actual stored file size of each page, and the estimated download times for various Internet connection speeds. The color-coded indicators to the left of each page tell you the following information about the connection speeds:

◇ Green means that the page loads quickly, within acceptable speed limits.

◇ Yellow means that the size of a page may make it load more slowly than desired.

◇ Red means that the size of a page is too large to load at an acceptable speed on a slower connection.

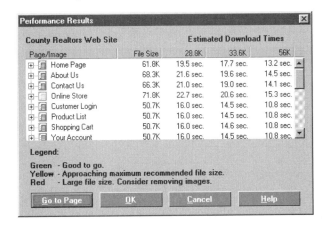

5. Review any yellow entries to find places where you can shorten text and reduce images, and review red entries to consider deleting images and reducing text in order to improve the speed at which the page loads.

6. Repeat the Performance Test.

Using Final Checklist

The Final Checklist option checks your Web project for completeness, and will warn you when default text or images or other problems appear.

To go through the Final Checklist, follow these steps:

1. From WebSite Complete with your Web project open, click the Final Steps tab in Control Panel.

2. Click the Final Checklist button.

3. The Final Checklist wizard runs and reports the results back to you (whether specific options pass or fail). When they pass, they're ready; when they fail, they need to be revised before you publish. The wizard checks for the following items:

⬦ For Default Text, you'll see a "Failed" response if default text (text placed on the page by WebSite Complete) has not been changed or deleted from your project.

⬦ For Default Images, you'll see a "Failed" response if default images (the placeholders for images WebSite Complete builds into your site template) have not been deleted or replaced.

⬦ For Contact Information, you'll see a "Failed" response if the contact information for your site is missing or incomplete.

⬦ For Search Engine Keywords & Description, you'll see a "Failed" response if you haven't filled out the search words and description identified in the previous section.

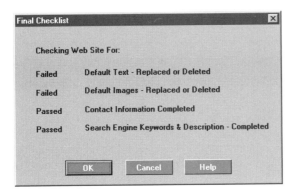

4. Click OK, and either return to your Web project to make desired changes and rerun the Final Checklist, or proceed to the next section.

Setting Up Your Domain and Web Hosting Account

In the following sections, you'll go through the process of registering your desired domain name for your Web site and setting up a hosting account. You can do this using your Web browser, or you can use an automated wizard provided in WebSite Complete to do both processes through the software itself.

You can register a domain name with Go Daddy Software for use with your site, even if you use another Web host provider. To set up a hosting account through the software, you can only do so using Go Daddy. If this is the case for you, use your Web browser to visit the Web host provider's site to obtain the information you need and set up your account before trying to publish.

Registering Your Domain

Although you checked for a good domain name as you planned your e-commerce site in Chapter 3, it's a wise idea to check the domain again before you try to register, especially if more than a day or two has elapsed (see step 4 in the following procedure).

To register a domain name with Go Daddy, for example, you have a choice: You can do it through an automated wizard in the WebSite Complete software when you set up your account in the next section, or you can use your Web browser to do it in advance of publishing your site. To do the latter, follow these steps:

1. Load your Web browser, connect to the Internet, and go to www.godaddy.com.

2. Click the Register a Domain Name link.

3. If this is your first time on Go Daddy's site to set up an account, you will be prompted to type in a username and password. You'll then be asked for your name and address.

   If you've already set up an account, type your username and password in the Existing Users logon section. Click Continue.

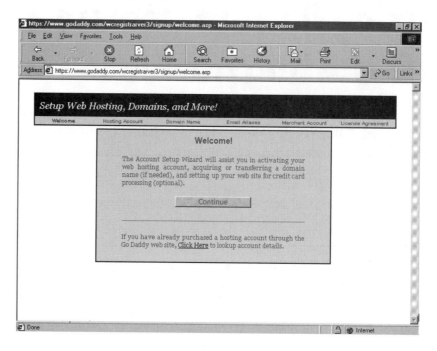

4. You'll then be prompted to check again for your domain name's availability. When you find an available domain you want to register, click Continue.

5. On the next screen, choose the length of time (in years) you want to register this domain. Often, the longer a period of time you agree to register this domain, the less it will cost you per year. You may

want to register for just one year, however, if you're only interested in testing the viability of an e-commerce site for your business. Click Continue.

6. On the Create Your Contact Information screen, fill out your name, e-mail address, company name, street address, city, state, zip code, country, primary phone number, and fax number (if applicable). Click Submit.

7. The next screen provides a menu from which you can choose to fill in more contact information, if, for example, another person acts as the contact for technical, administrative, and billing purposes. Click to choose one and fill out the information if you need to do so, or click Continue if you're the only person to be listed.

8. From the DNS Data/Domain Name page, click to choose from the following:

Option	What It Means
This domain will not be hosted anywhere.	Do not use.
I don't have a hosting provider yet. I'll park it here.	Parking is the act of setting up a domain name for possible future use but leaving it with a Web host on inactive status.
I will be using Go Daddy Software as my hosting domain.	Use this if you're about to set up a hosting account with Go Daddy.
I'm hosting with another ISP. I'll enter my information below.	This means you're registering the domain name for use with another Web hosting service. If you choose this, you must also provide the name server of the host you are using in the dialog box at the bottom of this information box. The name server is a unique identifier for the Web host provider, and it can be obtained from your Web host provider or from the information you received when you set up this account with the provider.

129

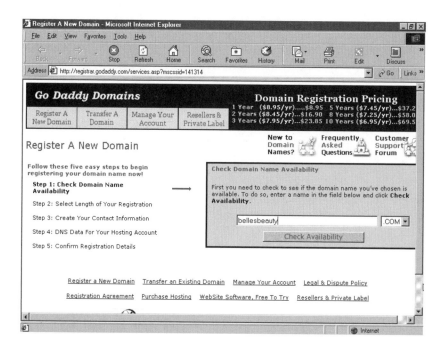

Click Continue.

9. Review your billing information. Click Continue.

10. A Shopping Cart screen will appear, with the price based on the length of registration you selected in step 5. Click Continue with Check Out.

11. Review your Customer and Shipping Information for accuracy; make changes as necessary. Click Continue with Check Out.

12. On the Order and Total Purchase screen, fill in the name on the credit card being used, the card number, the type (Visa, MasterCard, American Express, or Discover), and the expiration date of the card. Click Complete Your Purchase.

Be patient. This last step may take a few moments to complete before you receive a confirmation notice, which alerts you to look for an e-mail informing you of the successful registration of your domain name.

To begin managing your domain, click the Manage Your Account link on the Web page or click the Purchase Hosting link to set up a Web hosting account with Go Daddy (see the next section).

Establishing Your Web Hosting Account

Before you can publish your site, you need to set up an account with a Web service provider, also known as a Web host. You don't have to use Go Daddy to use WebSite Complete, but you may find it's easier to do so. If you set up an account with another Web host and then run into problems, it may be unclear whether you need to contact Go Daddy (for issues surrounding the Web software) or your Web host (for difficulties in publishing to the Web or accessing that Web). Also, WebSite Complete automates the publishing process for you to a greater extent with Go Daddy than if you use another Web host.

The process for signing up for a Web hosting account differs from provider to provider, but most follow the same basic steps. You must give the provider the domain name you want to use (and most help you register one if you haven't already done so), possibly answer questions about the kinds of extra features or services you may need, and provide both contact and billing information (usually a credit card).

If you set up your hosting account with Go Daddy, you can do so one of two ways: directly through the software or by visiting their Web site at www.godaddy.com and clicking the Web Site Hosting link. Use the latter method if you experience any difficulty with using the wizard in WebSite Complete itself.

Signing Up with WebSite Complete

WebSite Complete has a wizard built in to the software to help you set up an account with Go Daddy for Web hosting. To use this method, follow these steps:

1. From WebSite Complete, click the Final Steps tab in Control Panel.

2. Under Web Site Hosting & Domain Address Setup, click the Start button.

3. Click the Connect to the Internet button on the Web Site Registration Wizard screen to automatically connect.

Note

If this doesn't work, use whatever method you usually use to connect to the Internet and then click the Connect to the Internet button again. If this still fails, you can use the second method outlined in the following graphic.

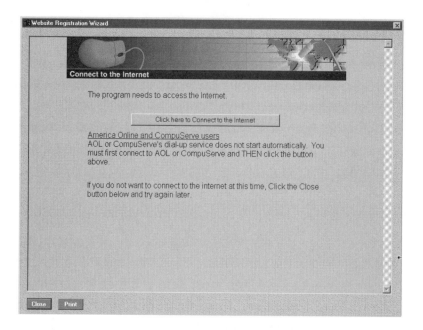

4. From the Welcome screen of the Account Setup Wizard, you're prompted to enter your Hosting/Discount ID. Unless you already have one to provide, click Continue without filling in an ID. (If you have already set up a hosting account and domain name with Go Daddy, click the Click Here link.)

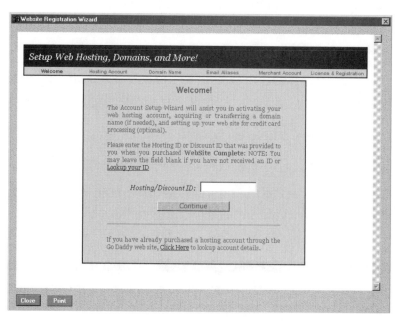

5. In the next screen, type in the username and password you want to use to access your new account. Type the password again to confirm it. Click Continue.

6. If you haven't already registered a domain, you can do so here by providing the name of the domain you want to use in the right side of the screen and clicking Check Availability. Then follow steps 2–12 in the previous section for registering your domain name.

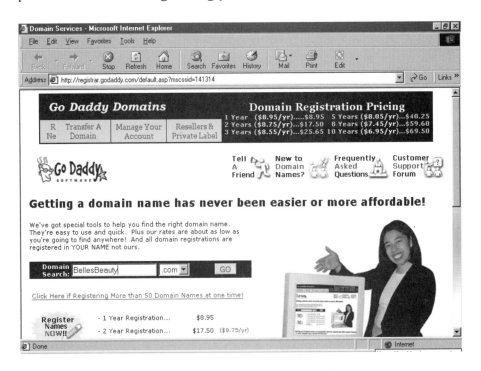

Or, if you've already registered your domain name, type the name of the domain you have registered in the dialog box on the right side of the screen and click Continue.

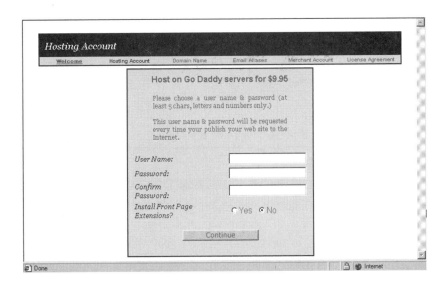

Warning

If you choose to host your Web site with Go Daddy, be aware that you'll pay more than just the monthly hosting fee of $9.95 and the domain registration of $8.95 per year (or less for a longer term). Normally, Go Daddy charges $49.95 for the one-time licensing of your WebSite Complete software at the time you post your first Web site to their server (subsequently added sites are $29.95 each). In a special arrangement with Go Daddy and this book's publisher, you will be able to get this one-time licensing at a $10 discount, or for $39.95.

You will now be led through the process of setting up your account:

1. First, you need to provide some information. Under Domain Name, type in the name of the domain you've registered, such as **onespecialclick.com**.

2. Check one of the following options to show how you obtained your domain:

   ◇ Choose New Domain if it's one you've just established.

   ◇ Choose Transferring a Domain if it's one you have registered in the past, perhaps with another Web service, and want to move it to Go Daddy for hosting.

   ◇ Choose Parked at Go Daddy if you jumped ahead in Chapter 3 to register an available domain and had Go Daddy park (hold) the site for you until you were ready to use it.

3. Under Hosting Account Login, type in a username and password (must be a minimum of five characters) to allow you access to your Web site hosting account.

4. Under Web Master's Contact Information, type in the full name, phone number, and e-mail address for the person responsible for your Web site and your hosting account (usually you).

5. Click Continue.

Tip

If you don't have a regular e-mail address or you would like to use a different e-mail address for the purposes of your Web site, you can sign up for a free Web-based e-mail account through Go Daddy or through services like MSN's Hotmail® at www.hotmail.com or Mail.com at www.mail.com.

6. Next, you'll see a screen for filling in up to five free e-mail addresses tied to your domain name (for example, `webmaster@onespecialclick.com`). These five accounts can be either POP3 accounts or aliases. Fill in the e-mail addresses you want to use, following the examples provided. Note that Go Daddy forwards mail that comes into these domain Web accounts only to the e-mail address you provided on the first screen.

    Click Finished when you're done.

7. A prompt will now ask you whether or not you want to sign up for a merchant account. You can click Apply to do so now, or click Don't Apply to wait until you read more about it in Chapter 9, "Building Your Online Store."

    If you checked Apply, click Yes to agree to the license agreement.

8. From the Shopping Cart screen that appears, review your order for one month of Web hosting. If everything checks out, click Check Out to continue. If not, click Empty Cart to stop and start over.

9. From the Customer and Shipping Information screen, verify that your information is correct and click Continue with Check Out.

10. From the next Shopping Cart page, provide your credit card type (MasterCard, Visa, American Express, or Discover), credit card number, and expiration date; then click Complete Your Purchase.

Once you've done this, you'll receive a purchase confirmation giving you a receipt number, customer number, account password, the e-mail address you supplied, and a note indicating your account will be set up within the next business day (Monday through Friday).

Hosting Through Go Daddy Software

If you host your account through Go Daddy, what do you get for the hosting fee of $9.95 that you pay them monthly?

- ◇ No monthly setup fee (many hosts do charge an initial setup fee)
- ◇ Monthly billing (no long-term commitment required), which is automatically charged to your credit card
- ◇ Access to Web usage reports for your site
- ◇ Up to 50MB of publishing space, which far exceeds what a typical small business site would use
- ◇ Support for up to five e-mail accounts tied to your domain name

Using Another Web Host

You can choose to use a Web host other than Go Daddy, but you won't be able to take advantage of some of the special features (like plug-ins), and you can't use the online store builder component of the software to prepare an e-commerce site. The online store feature is first developed on your hard drive as you work with WebSite Complete, but only becomes a capable online store when published to your Web site through operations performed on Go Daddy's servers.

Tip

Print this confirmation page and keep it in a safe, secure location in case you need the information at a later time.

name server

a computer that contains a list of domain names and their corresponding IP addresses (like 63.241.136.30); when you type a domain name into a Web browser and you try to connect to the site, it's the job of the name server to associate that domain name with its IP address to make sure the correct Web site opens in the Web browser

You can return to the Go Daddy site at any time and click the Your Account option to review your account information or change your password.

If you choose to use a different Web provider, make certain you have the name of your Web host's **name server**—you'll need this to publish. This information can be obtained from your Web host, or it may be contained in the e-mail confirming your hosting account.

Posting Your Web Site to the Server

Follow these steps to publish your site to your Web server:

1. With WebSite Complete open to the project you want to publish to your e-commerce site, choose the Final Steps tab from Control Panel.

2. Locate the Publish Your Web to the Internet field in the middle of the screen and click Start.

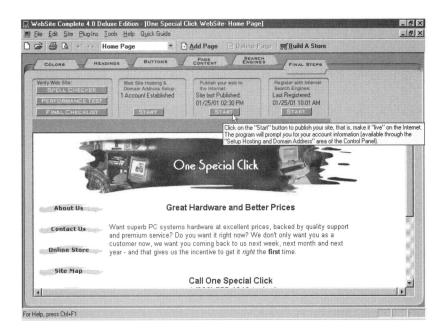

3. Click the Connect to the Internet button.

4. When prompted, provide your username and password.

Your site will then be published to your Web server. Remember to load your Web browser and check that your site has published and that it appears as you intended. If you identify problems you need to correct, you'll learn how to do so in the next chapter.

Note

If you're just setting up your domain and account names, you may not be able to publish immediately, as it takes time for the domain and site to be set up. Or, if you can publish, you may not be able to access the live site (because it's not yet live) until the domain and site account are properly established.

WebSite Complete also supports a feature called smart posting. This differs from the regular publishing procedure in that after the first time you publish your Web project to the Web host server, you can choose to upload only modifications made to your site since the last time you published. This can save you time in the publishing process, because time isn't being wasted uploading pages and images that haven't changed. You'll learn more about this in the next chapter.

Chapter 7

Revising Your Published E-Commerce Site

Once you review and test your published e-commerce site, it's time to make any revisions you find necessary or desirable. Some changes may show up only when you begin reviewing and testing the site after you've published it. You will either catch a typo you didn't see earlier or notice a problem with one of the online-only components, like a Loan Payment Calculator or a hit counter.

With WebSite Complete, the editing process is very much like the creation process from Chapter 4, "Building Your First E-Commerce Web Site," because you're using the same tools. And because a copy of your entire e-commerce site is stored on the hard disk of your computer, you can make those changes locally (without being online to do so) and get them right *before* you upload them again to the site. This way, if you can't do all your modifications at once and don't want to publish them piecemeal, your changes won't show up on the site until you finish all changes and republish the site.

Testing Your Site

If you do want to make modifications a bit at a time and have the changes you make in each session immediately reflected on your site, you have the option to republish each time as soon as you finish working. It should take no more than a few minutes to do with a basic e-commerce Web site and up to several minutes for a site with many pages added.

This chapter will show you how to test and review your site, make any desired or necessary changes, and republish the site.

Once you publish your e-commerce site for the first time, you should use your Web browser to load the site, as visitors will, and review it carefully. If possible, encourage friends or colleagues to do the same and to share their feedback with you.

As you conduct your review, look for the following problems:

- ◆ pages that load too slowly or don't load at all
- ◆ pages where font or background color makes it difficult to read the text
- ◆ images on pages that either don't display or lose all their detail
- ◆ typos and grammatical errors
- ◆ missing information
- ◆ links that don't work
- ◆ features, such as a Loan Payment Calculator, that don't work

As you work, make a list of problems found or reported to you so that you can make the needed changes.

Modifying Web Site Content

You already know the basic steps in modifying **content** (text, images, and pages) from setting up your first e-commerce site in Chapter 4, "Building Your First E-Commerce Web Site." (You should review the chapter if you don't recall details.) You'll learn how to make modifications to your online store in Chapter 9, "Building Your Online Store."

content
the meat and potatoes of any Web site, including any text or images that have been created especially for the site, but not including the templates that were designed to lay out the pages

As you modify your content, remember that you cannot recover pages that you delete from your Web site project. Be sure you no longer want to include a page—or *any* of its content—before you remove it. The one exception to this is if you use the Backup option in WebSite Complete to store a copy of your Web project prior to deleting the page you want to recover. If so, follow these steps to restore the previous version of this project (bearing in mind that it won't reflect any changes you've made since deleting the page):

1. Click the File menu and either select Restore or press Ctrl+R.

2. From the Backup and Restore Project window, scan the list of Available Backup Projects on the left side of the screen and select the one you want to reinstate.

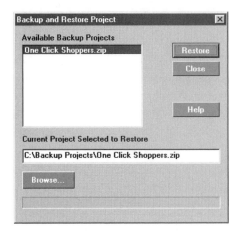

3. Click Restore.

The backup copy of your Web project, which was zipped automatically by the software to store it in a smaller form, is then unzipped and placed in the appropriate folder (a folder under WebSite Complete named for the project's own name). It should then open from this folder in WebSite Complete after prompting you that the restore process was a success.

Tip

If you make a mistake as you work that you want to undo immediately without much fuss, click the Edit option on the WebSite Complete menu bar and select Undo. If you undo something in error, go back to Edit and choose Redo.

Repairing Broken Links

broken link

a link on a Web site that, when clicked, fails to produce the desired results (the Web page it's meant to open does not load)

Each time you revise your site, it's important to be sure that all the links that appear on your Web site pages still work, meaning that they point to the correct page on your site or another site and, when clicked, will bring up the page for viewing.

Broken links are a common problem on Web sites and can easily frustrate visitors. It may lead some visitors to believe that this business site isn't very well maintained and wonder what else may not work.

To modify a link on your site, perform these steps:

1. With your Web site open, right-click the link you want to modify.

2. From the menu, choose Link Image To.

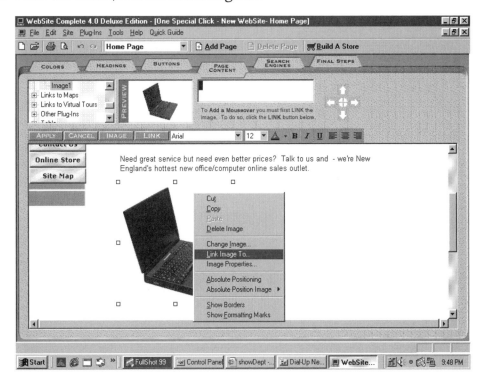

3. From the Link To screen, choose either of the following options:

   ❖ URL to type in the name of the correct Web address for the site or a page on another site

   ❖ *or*, Page in Your Web Site to select from the drop-down list the page on your site in which this link should open

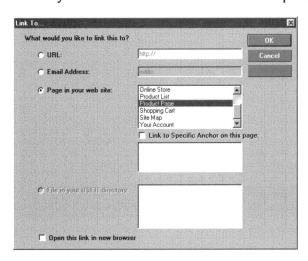

4. Click OK.

To remove a link altogether, perform these steps instead:

1. With your Web site open, right-click the link you want to remove.

2. Select Link Image To.

3. From the Link To screen, choose Remove Link.

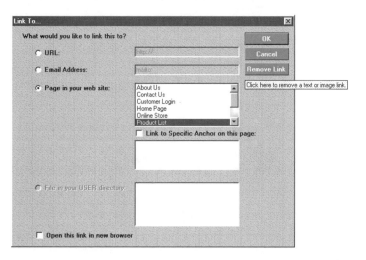

Pesky 404 Errors

If you're using Internet Explorer, for example, and click a hyperlink to open a new page, you may receive an HTTP 404 Error. This browser error occurs when IE cannot find the site—or page on a site—that should be the destination of the link. This may be because the page is no longer available (for example, a specific page has been deleted) or because the link is incorrect or misspelled.

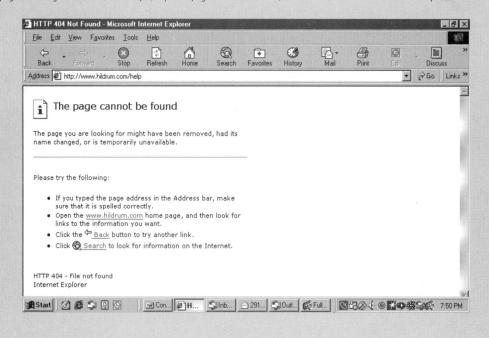

Warning

Don't just verify links to pages within your own site if you're also including links to external sites (other company sites, for example). All links used should be checked both before and regularly after publishing.

Verifying Your Web Site

When you first published your site, you went through the final steps on the Final Steps tab in WebSite Complete's Control Panel. You will now do this again just before you post to check your site for spelling errors, the completeness of your site, and the speed at which pages load for visitors. (See the previous chapter for details.)

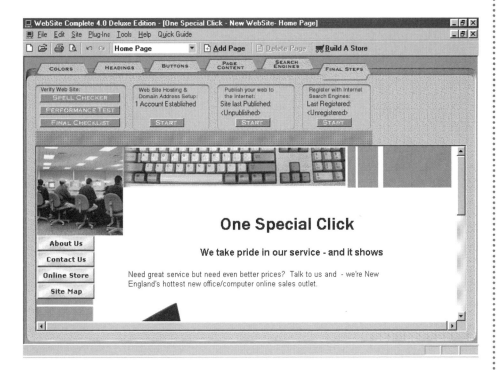

You should repeat these steps before you publish any changes you've made since you first published your site. You may think you caught everything, but you can save yourself work later in case a page you modified now comes up too slowly or you mistyped something during editing.

Republishing Your Site Changes

Once your modifications are complete, you need to republish your Web project to your Web host in order for those changes to be available to those who visit your e-commerce site.

Republishing is very much like publishing the site for the first time, except that you've already done the detail work of setting up an account and testing it to be sure it works. However, you should make a habit of reviewing it again yourself before you republish (so a mistake doesn't make you go through it a third time), as well as performing both a spell check and a performance test—unless the changes you make are very insignificant.

Follow these steps to republish your site:

1. With WebSite Complete open to the project you've modified, choose the Final Steps tab from Control Panel.

2. Locate the Publish Your Web to the Internet field in the middle of the screen and click Start.

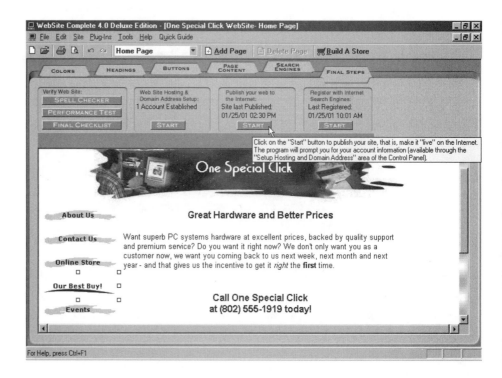

3. When prompted, provide your username and password.

Your site will then be republished to your Web server, and the changes will appear for those visiting your Web site.

Be sure to review your site once again to be sure all the modifications you make appear as you expect. If not, you can repeat the process. If your changes don't show up shortly after republishing your site (in fact, the changes should be applied as soon as the publishing session finishes), be sure to click the Refresh button on your Web browser to freshly load the page in the browser. This may be necessary because of **page caching**.

Using Smart Posting

When you make modifications to your site, you're usually modifying only a few pages at once or perhaps only exchanging one image for another. You, there-fore, wouldn't need to republish your entire site.

If you're making just a few modifications, you can use a WebSite Complete feature called **smart posting**. You will usually save at least some time using this method, because you don't have to transfer as much data from the Web project on your hard drive to the Web server. For instance, if you're only making changes to text and your site features several images, you save all the time it takes to upload those images again unnecessarily—and images usually take the most time to transfer.

Smart posting isn't a separate tool: You can choose it any time you republish your site to your Web host server. Here's how:

1. With WebSite Complete open to the Web project you want to republish, click the Final Steps tab in Control Panel.

page caching
depending on how your browser has been configured for use, revisiting a site may cause the site to load from a copy stored on your hard drive from the last session, not from the Web server itself

smart posting
a method in which you publish only the pages or files of your site that have been changed since you last published

2. Click the Start button directly beneath the Publish Your Web to the Internet field.

3. From the Confirmation pop-up window, choose Upload Only Modified/New Files.

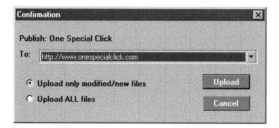

4. Click Upload.

The files that changed as a result of your modifications then begin transferring to your Web host server (as shown below) where these changes will be made available to visitors to your Web site.

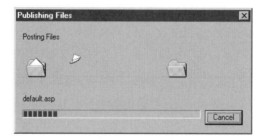

Chapter 8

Diagnosing and Curing Common Web Site Problems

T he best troubleshooting technique for keeping your e-commerce site accessible and in good working condition is a proactive one, where you're checking your site to catch problems before potential customers run into them. Visitors to your site may not let you know if they have a problem, even if you give them a way to do so. They may instead go away discouraged by their inability to either access your site or properly order products or services.

Thus, it's wise to check your own site on a regular basis to make certain that it opens promptly for access and that there are no difficulties reaching the links from your home page. Occasionally, if you're running an online store, go as far as you can in the order submission process—without actually processing the order—to verify that online ordering is working correctly as well.

Problems Accessing Your Site

Almost every Web site becomes temporarily unavailable at some point. Access problems may result from a problem with your Internet connection, a failed publishing effort, a technical difficulty occurring with your Web host provider, or a problem with a major leg of networks running Internet connections. Such outages can last minutes or even stretch into days, depending on the size of the problem.

If you find that you can't reach your site through your Internet connection and your Web browser, it's therefore likely that you will not be able to publish updates to your site.

If you have problems accessing your site, first try disconnecting from your Internet session and then connecting again. Often, a bad connection—and these can be caused by sudden line noise, a problem with your Internet service provider, or other problems—can cause short-term problems. If you still have difficulty, try another Internet account or a different access number for the same Internet account.

If you still can't access the site, try calling a friend or colleague and ask them to try. If they can't reach it either, contact your Web host provider and advise them of the problems immediately. While it's likely that they'll already know about the difficulty if it's a problem with their equipment or an issue with the Internet itself, it's wise to wait no more than a few hours before you contact them. It's even possible that the issue can be easily corrected in a few minutes' time. You just never know how many good potential customers you can miss during downtime.

Even though you should promptly report any problem you experience, you need to be realistic, too. Unless your provider specifically offers support for Web access problems 24/7, you may have to wait until at least the next business day for a response.

It's important to know whom to contact as well. For example, if you're having a problem using or publishing with WebSite Complete, contact Go Daddy Software through their support message boards. If you're having a problem connecting to your Web host provider, publishing, or even just viewing your site—and you're using a different Web host provider than Go Daddy—contact your provider.

Tip

If you find that your Web host provider seems to go down often—meaning that they have a lot of problems keeping their system consistently up and available around the clock—discuss the issues with them. If they have no plan in place to fix the problem in a timely fashion, consider finding yourself a new Web host provider. Most professional Web hosts have equipment in place to take over the work when the main system fails.

Problems Publishing to Your Site

If you encounter difficulty when connecting through WebSite Complete to publish to your site, load your Web browser and try to access it as a visitor does. If you can't connect this way, contact your Web site host. You probably won't be able to publish until the problem at their end or beyond (a problem with one of the traffic routes on the Internet itself, for example) is corrected.

You may find yourself in a situation where you disconnect in the middle of a publishing session. This can happen when WebSite Complete loses contact with your Web host provider, or it may happen for other reasons, such as disconnection from your ISP or a problem on your line (someone picking up an extension phone on the same line).

Try these steps to get back to publishing:

1. If WebSite Complete is responding, click Start/Publish again to try to reconnect to the Internet and recommence publishing.

2. If step 1 is unsuccessful, exit WebSite Complete, reload it, and again try to publish.

3. If step 2 fails, exit WebSite Complete again and close all other programs. Then choose Windows Start ➢ Shut Down ➢ Restart. Once the system restarts and resets hardware (like the modem you may have installed in your system), try step 2 again.

 Note

Some services, like America Online© and CompuServe©, will require you to reconnect manually to your service before you try to publish. If you don't get a response when you click the Connect to the Internet button immediately after clicking Publish, connect using your usual dial-up method (for example, load and connect via your America Online software), wait until the connection is established, and then click Connect to the Internet.

Problems Using Your Site

Even though you review and test your site, problems can crop up on their own. For example, a page may become corrupted or damaged on the server and need replacement. Problems can also be caused by an error you make in revising a Web page for republishing.

 Warning

Remember that changes you make to your disk-based Web project won't be reflected on your Web site until you republish the project to your Web host.

Pages Loading Too Slowly

When a page loads too slowly, it typically means that the page size exceeds what can be transmitted in a reasonable time frame given the speed at which you, or a visitor to your site, connect to the Internet.

From Chapter 6, "Publishing Your E-Commerce Web Site," you know the importance of taking the site performance review step before you publish. You also know that you should use the WebSite Complete Performance Test tool to see which pages are loading too slowly by those reported as yellow or red. Therefore, when a page loads too slowly, it could mean that you skipped the performance review or that you didn't fix a potential problem.

Images are most often the culprit, because they tend to be larger in file size than text or HTML and require more storage room for finer details.

Images on Web sites are commonly used in one of these graphics formats:

- GIF (for CompuServe's Graphics Interchange Format) format is limited to using 256 colors, but it can save an image file in 10–20 percent of its original file size.

- JPG, or JPEG, (Joint Photographic Experts Group) format offers better compression than GIF (images can be compressed down to as little as 5–10 percent of their original size), but it loses some of the details.

- BMP (for Windows Bitmap Protocol) format is usually used for wallpaper or background on your Windows Desktop or a Web site.

- PNG (Portable Network Graphics) format is fairly new (and used by WebSite Complete). Supported by both Netscape and Internet Explorer, it's designed to replace GIF, which uses a copyrighted data-compression method.

Working with Images

You don't have to be a graphics master to work with images on your Web site. Free Web art is available to download and use from hundreds, if not thousands, of locations on the Web. The decreasing cost and better performance of today's **digital cameras** make it reasonably affordable for you to create your own artwork and save it in a format that can be used on your Web site.

If you work a lot with images or need to change the graphics format of pictures you have saved into another format for use on your Web site, you'll want to get a good graphics program to help you. For example, Paint Shop Pro™ 7 is one that's available for a free 30-day trial just by downloading it from Jasc® Software's site at **www.jasc.com**.

digital camera
a type of camera that saves pictures to electronic media, such as a smart card (looks like a tiny disk), rather than to film that must be developed

Since WebSite Complete's templates lay out a suggested placement and quantity of images, you should check to see if you added several extra images to one of your pages. If you did, review your inclusions to see what can be deleted or moved to a different page on your site (refer to the techniques in Chapter 3, "Planning Your First E-Commerce Site").

For best results, the smallest image file size possible (10–20K) should be used, particularly when a page features more than a few images. Check the file size of the images you've used. Images—or combinations of images—of 100K or larger should be used as little as possible. You'll learn more about this in a discussion of digital photography in Chapter 9, "Building Your Online Store."

Follow these steps to determine the file size of your images:

1. From Windows Start, point to Programs ➢ Windows Explorer.

2. From Windows Explorer, browse through the Folders list. Find and select for viewing the location of the images you're using for your Web site.

3. Click a filename in the list on the right.

4. See the bottom of the Windows Explorer window for the size of the file.

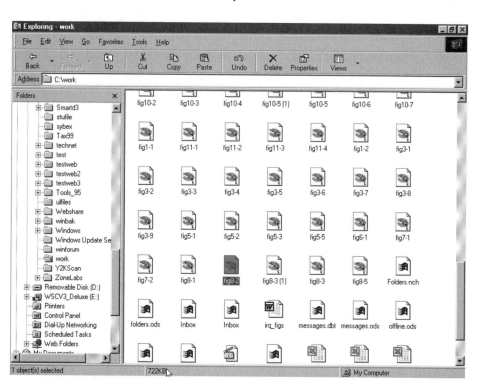

Or, you can right-click the filename and choose Properties to display the filename and type, the location of the file, its size, its dates of creation and modification, and the method used to save the file to your disk.

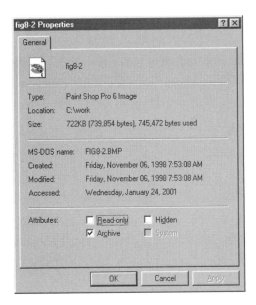

You can accomplish the same thing using WebSite Complete:

1. With your Web project open, right-click an image used in your Web project and choose Change Image.

2. In the bottom left of the Select an Image screen, note the information about the image being used, including file size.

Difficulty Seeing or Reading Pages

If you find it hard to make out details or see the text on one of your pages, it's usually because the specialized colors you're using for fonts or custom color schemes for templates don't work well together. If so, you'll need to go back and change the font or custom template colors so that they will be more easily read (see Chapter 3).

You should avoid using a font color that is too close to the background color being used, such as pale blue text on a darker blue background. Also avoid using colors that are difficult to see because they clash (orange text on a purple background). PC video adapters can differ widely in the colors they present, so what may be clearly visible to you when you publish may not be clearly visible to a visitor.

Once you modify the colors, fonts, and template custom colors as necessary, republish and recheck your results.

E-Mail Not Working

There are many types of e-mail software you can use (for example, Microsoft® Outlook® Express available with Microsoft Internet Explorer, Microsoft Outlook, Netscape® Communicator, and Eudora™). How you resolve problems with e-mail not reaching you depends on which software you use and who you use as your Web provider.

If you're hosting your Web site through Go Daddy, any mail that you receive in the five possible e-mail accounts tied to your domain is forwarded to your regular e-mail account through your online service or ISP.

Follow these steps to check any links from your pages to your e-mail:

1. With your Web project open, right-click the link you want to check.

2. Select Change Link To.

3. Verify the e-mail address typed there; modify as necessary.

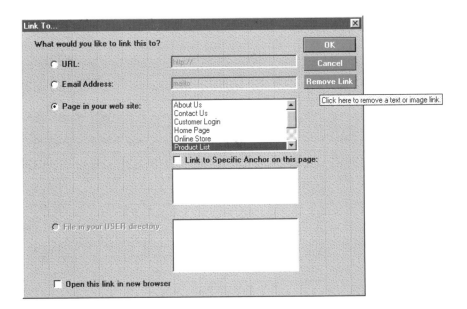

Problems with a Page after Adding HTML

You may find that the extra HTML code added to one of your Web pages doesn't either display correctly or work as it should. The best way to proceed is to remove the HTML code and then republish the site so that it reflects the modification. You can always add it again later, if desired, once you figure out the problem with the code. After all, it's more important that your pages open and work correctly than it is to have the HTML code in place, at least in the short term.

If you "borrowed" code from another Web site, consider asking the Web master of that site to provide some insight into why it doesn't work for you. You can usually contact the Web master by addressing e-mail to webmaster@*sitename*.com, where "*sitename*" is the name of the Web site.

Pages Looking Different in Netscape

Small variations exist between a Web page viewed in Microsoft Internet Explorer and one viewed in Netscape Navigator, and these variations can be exaggerated when using older versions of either browser. Usually, these differences are quite slight and most often affect exact colors, fonts, and, to some degree, formatting.

Also, much older versions of Netscape may either fail to display the scrolling marquee plug-in with WebSite Complete or display it only as an unmoving header.

For best results and for your own peace of mind, you can check your e-commerce site with Netscape immediately after each time you publish your site to make sure a page that looks fine in IE also looks fine in Netscape. If you don't have the Netscape browser and want to check for compatibility, you can download a copy from Netscape at `www.netscape.com`.

When necessary, you can modify the colors, fonts, and template custom colors, and then republish and recheck your results.

Tip

Many Web sites include a brief recommendation that users upgrade to the latest version of their Web browsers, and they may even provide a link to download the latest versions of the two major browsers, Internet Explorer and Netscape Navigator. This can prompt users to upgrade their older browsers and therefore limit the amount of difficulties they may encounter when accessing your site.

Images Not Displaying after Publishing

Sometimes you will see a small red "x" or other placeholder where the actual image should be visible. Most often, this isn't a problem with your published pages, but with the settings in the browser being used to view the page.

To be sure it's not a temporary problem (some pages may load slowly or erratically), click the Refresh button on your Web browser. This forces the page to fully reload and, it is hoped, restore the image(s).

If you still can't see images on Web sites other than your own, and you're using Windows 98 or later, follow these steps:

1. Close your Web browser.

2. From Windows Start, point to Programs ➢ Accessories ➢ System Tools.

3. Select Disk Cleanup.

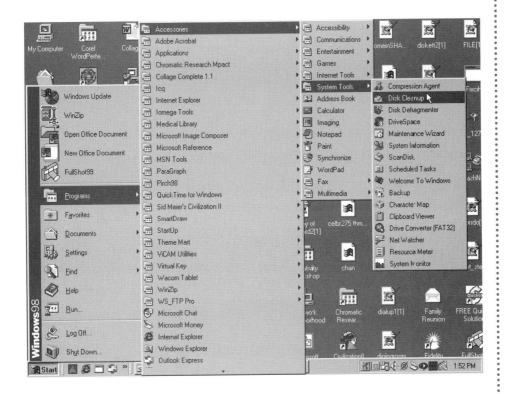

4. Choose the letter of the disk you want to clean (usually the C drive).

5. From the Disk Cleanup window, make certain that Temporary Internet Files is selected. (If it's not selected, click to check it.) Click OK.

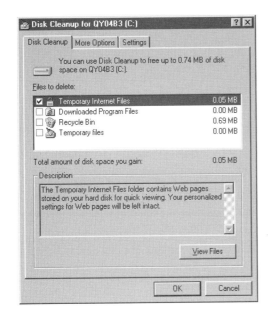

6. Load your browser and try again to access your Web site to see if the images now display. If not, continue to step 7.

7. Disconnect from your Internet service and try to reconnect (a temporary problem with your connection may be the problem).

If you still have no luck displaying the images, you may want to shut down and restart your system, connect to the Internet, and then try again.

Finally, check your browser to be sure you don't have it set to ignore image files. Here's how to check:

1. From Windows Start, point to Settings ➤ Control Panel.

2. Double-click the Internet Options icon and choose the Advanced tab.

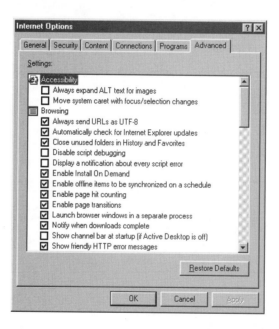

3. Scroll down to the section labeled Multimedia and make sure the Show Pictures check box is checked. (If not, check it.) Click OK.

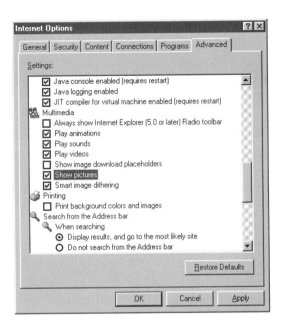

You may be prompted to restart your system. If you are, do so and then try to load your Web site in the browser.

If images are still not visible, try another Web site where you know images are located (such as CNN™ at www.cnn.com). If you can see the images on another site but not on yours, go back into WebSite Complete and reverify the images. If necessary, delete the images and reinsert them, then publish again and recheck.

Buttons Having the Wrong Text

If buttons have the wrong text displayed after you've made modifications to your site, you will need to change the text on the buttons to correspond with the revisions you made.

Follow these steps to do this:

1. With WebSite Complete open to the page (or one of the pages in the project), click the Buttons tab in Control Panel.

2. In the Edit window at the upper right of the Preview pane, click the current text and change it to the text you now want to display.

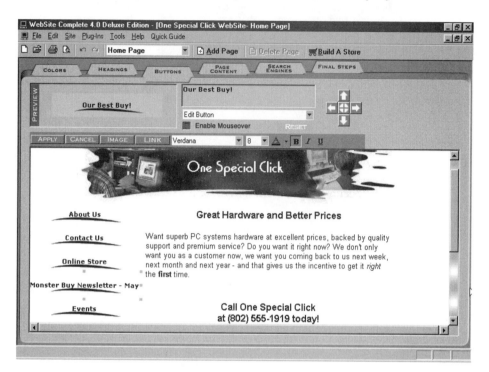

3. Check your results in the Preview window before you republish the change.

Chapter 9

Building Your Online Store

The process for building an online store begins on your PC using WebSite Complete. The information for this store is saved in a database format, which is uploaded as you publish your whole e-commerce site. Go Daddy's servers then take that database information and create the actual virtual store for you, organizing your products and store data.

Your customers will be able to see the products and departments in your online store, use a Shopping Cart tool to store their online purchases until checkout, and provide their payment information for almost instant approval and order processing by the vendor (you).

You will be able to access information compiled into reports about certain aspects of your site. For example, the Track Advertising feature allows you to track where the customer learned of your site, such as from an ad on a news site. Follow the steps in this chapter to build and track the success of your online store.

merchant account

a special type of Web hosting account that establishes your business' creditworthiness, and sets up a way for financial transactions to be performed on your site (such as the processing of credit card orders)

Using a Merchant Account

Easy online processing of orders and payments requires a **merchant account**. A merchant account gives you the ability to accept the credit cards that Go Daddy can process, such as MasterCard, Visa, American Express, and Discover, and then provide your customers with confirmation that their charges are approved. Thus, this confirms that their order is approved and you can ship it to them.

 Note

To use an online store, you'll need to have a merchant account with Go Daddy and use them as your Web host. You can build one as part of a project, but when you publish the project, you'll be prompted to apply for a merchant account.

Here's how online processing of credit cards through a Go Daddy merchant account works:

1. A customer visits your e-commerce site and online store (remember that your store's information was organized by Go Daddy when you published). The customer selects a product for purchase and provides their payment and billing/shipping information; Go Daddy's servers store this information.

2. Go Daddy's server then sends out a signal to a special electronic gateway that handles credit card approvals, indicating that it has an order to process (similar to using a credit card to pay at a store checkout).

3. When the electronic gateway is ready to process the transaction, Go Daddy passes the information to the gateway, which in turn passes the credit card information to the credit card–processing systems in a secure manner.

4. The credit card processors verify that the customer has enough available funds on their credit line to pay for the purchase. If enough is available, the processor holds that amount of money in reserve.

5. The credit card processors send a message back over the electronic gateway, saying whether this transaction has been approved or declined, and the electronic gateway passes this information back to Go Daddy as your merchant agent.

6. If the credit card was approved, Go Daddy's systems allow your e-commerce site to accept the order and notify you to process the physical order (accumulate the goods and ship them out).

   If the credit card was declined, Go Daddy's systems will report this back to the customer, along with any information provided as the reason the order was declined. It gives the customer the option to try to process the order again, try to place the order with a different credit card, or terminate the order.

7. At the end of each day, all successful credit card charges are settled through the issuing creditors (such as Visa), and the funds from each issuing creditor are deposited in the bank account you specify when you set up your merchant account. The money deposited to you is drawn from the available balance on the customer's credit card, where it had been on reserve since the transaction was approved.

Establishing a Merchant Account

You can set up your merchant account with Go Daddy either before you build your online store or when you first publish the online store you built in WebSite Complete. If you're in a hurry to publish, you may want to establish the account ahead of time so that there won't be any delay in publishing and offering your online store to the public while Go Daddy processes your application.

Follow these steps to apply for a merchant account:

1. Go to Go Daddy's site at www.godaddy.com using your Web browser.

2. Click the Merchant Accounts link on the left, and then click Apply Now.

3. Fill out the online Merchant Account application (includes information about you and your business, how settlements will be paid, etc.).

Warning

The Merchant Account application requires a good deal of detailed information about your business' credit rating, how payments (from the service through to your bank) will be processed, and other criteria for approval. It may be necessary for you to pose questions to Go Daddy (using the www.supportwebsite.com address discussed in Chapter 2, "Getting Started with WebSite Complete") and/or your financial institution in order to fully and accurately complete this form and submit it.

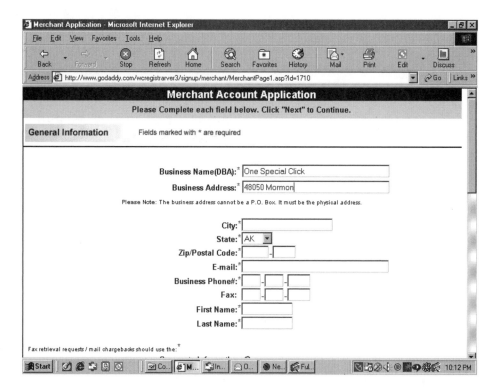

4. You will receive an e-mail containing various merchant account documents. Print them out, sign them, and return them to the address provided.

5. Check your e-mail over the next week (approximately) for an approval notification of your merchant account.

Warning

It may take a week or longer to be approved for a merchant account, so plan accordingly. Also, approval is not guaranteed; it's based on various criteria, as noted above.

Once your merchant account is approved, it must be activated through Go Daddy's Online Manager (more about Online Manager later in this chapter). Follow these steps to activate it:

1. Load your Web browser.

2. Type this address in your browser address bar: `http://www` `.yourdomainname.com/manager`. Press Enter.

3. When prompted, type in the domain name, username, and password you set up when establishing your Web hosting account with Go Daddy.

4. From Online Manager, click the Merchant Account Mgmt link.

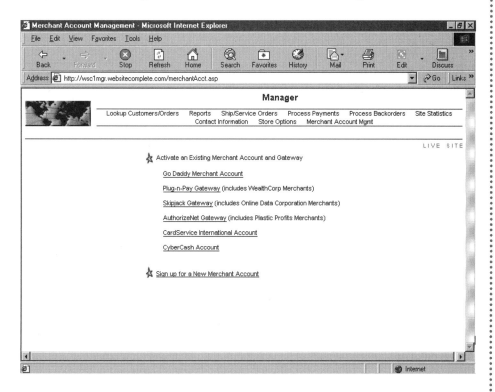

5. Type in the login identification (username and password) provided to you when your merchant account was approved (check your confirmation e-mail).

Setting Up Your Online Store

When you begin to build your online store, you'll notice that the E-Commerce Component window has many different parts, which either offer information or require information from you. Each of these parts or sections addresses a specific feature or tool for building your online store.

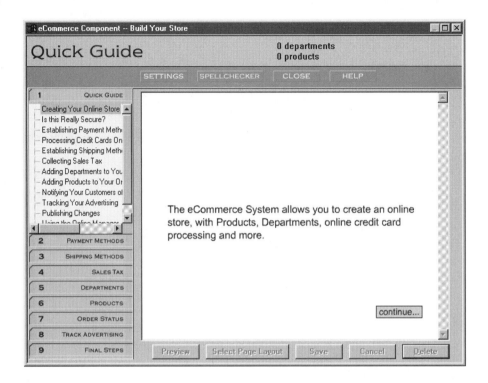

First, go through these short steps to start your online store and then go through each of the following sections separately to build your store.

Follow these steps:

1. With WebSite Complete loaded, click the File menu to open the Web site project to which to want to add a store.

2. Click the Build Online Store icon on the toolbar.

3. The E-Commerce Component window opens, and the toolbar at the top of the screen offers these options:

    ♦ Use Settings to configure settings for your e-commerce data entry.

    ♦ Use Spell Checker to verify the spelling in your e-commerce project.

    ♦ Use Close to exit the E-Commerce Component window and return to your project.

    ♦ Use Help to open the Help window for WebSite Complete.

4. Check the nine numbered step buttons at the left, including Quick Guide, Payment Methods, Shipping Methods, Sales Tax, Departments, Products, Order Status, Track Advertising, and Final Steps (see sections that follow for more details about these step buttons).

5. For each of the buttons from steps 3 and 4, fill them out as appropriate, based on a review of the information you will supply in the following sections.

6. Click Close to close the E-Commerce Component window and return to your Web project, now with an online store component added.

7. Publish your site, including its online store, following the information from later in this chapter.

Using the Settings and Spell Checker Buttons

These two options on the left of the toolbar in the E-Commerce Component window allow you to configure settings for online store entries and spell-check your online store data. Remember that the information, or data, for this store is saved in a **database** format, which is uploaded as you publish your e-commerce site.

database

a collection of information (data) that is organized on various key fields (product or customer name, for example) so that the stored data can be quickly retrieved

You can use the Settings option to modify your settings for entering data (products) into your online store. Follow these steps to use this option:

1. Click the Settings button on the E-Commerce Component window toolbar.

2. From the Settings window, click to select any of the following options that you want to use:

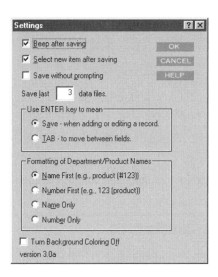

◇ Check Beep after Saving for a sound prompt that lets you know the entry has been saved.

❖ Check Select New Item after Saving so that, after a record is saved, it automatically produces a fresh record window to enter a new product.

❖ Check Save without Prompting to automate WebSite Complete to save the file automatically without your confirmation.

❖ In the Save Last [*number*] Data Files field, type in a new number to modify as desired.

❖ In the Use Enter Key to Mean field, choose either Save to save a record or Tab to move to the next field in a record.

❖ In the Formatting of Department/Product Names field, choose from Name First, Number First, Name Only, or Number Only.

❖ Check Turn Background Coloring Off to remove any coloring in the field where your product is displayed.

3. Click either OK to save your settings and return to the E-Commerce Component window or Cancel to exit the Settings window without saving.

You can click the Spell Checker button on the toolbar to launch an e-commerce version of WebSite Complete's spell checker, much as you did in Chapter 6, "Publishing Your E-Commerce Web Site," when you prepared your site for first publishing. Use this feature just before you save your e-commerce project and exit back to your Web project in WebSite Complete.

E-Commerce Setup Steps

The nine numbered step buttons on the left side of the E-Commerce Component window lay out the major steps necessary in developing your online store into a finished product you can publish. Click each button to expand the topics covered under each of the setup steps (from Quick Guide to Final Steps).

Step 1: Quick Guide Help for E-Commerce

The Quick Guide offers Quick Guide help sessions specific to building an online store and learning about the components available on the E-Commerce Component window. These guided help sessions can give you more information about the steps that you take in building or modifying your online store.

Step 2: Payment Methods

The Payment Methods step sets up information for online payment acceptance and processing. Click Payment Methods to see the tree listing of the basic payment methods you can use with your online store. Click each that applies to your site to enable that option on your site and provide any information as requested for each payment method.

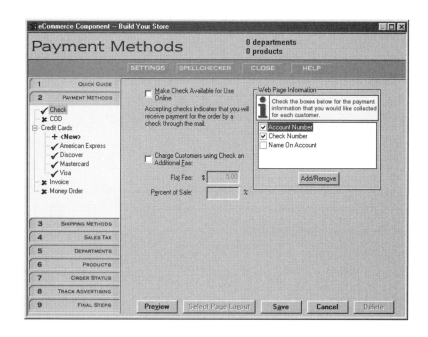

Major payment methods include the following:

❖ Clicking the Check option means that you will allow customers to place an order with you and then mail you a check to pay for the order prior to shipping.

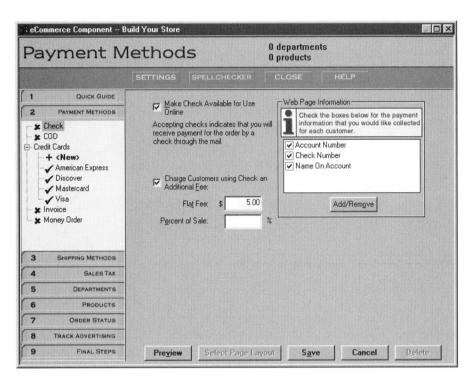

Further information is then required:

❖ Click to check Make Check Available for Use Online.

❖ Click to check if you want to charge an additional administrative fee for accepting a check, and then provide either the exact dollar amount to charge or the percentage of total sale to charge.

❖ Check the options at right (under Web Page Information) that you want to ask the customer to supply when choosing to pay by check (account number, check number, name on checking account), or click the Add/Remove button to bring up the Data Field Manager to modify your selections.

- Enabling the COD (Cash on Delivery) option allows customers to pay for the order at the time it's delivered. Further information is then required:

  - Click to check Make COD Available for Use Online.

  - Click to check if you want to charge an additional administrative fee for accepting COD for payment (such as to help cover COD cost), and then provide the exact dollar amount to charge or the percentage of total sale to charge.

  - Check the option at right under Web Page Information to let the customer select the Anyone May Sign option for delivery, or click the Add/Remove button to bring up the Data Field Manager to modify your selections.

Warning

If you choose to accept COD as a method of payment, you will need to complete forms necessary to collect the COD payment.

- Choose the Credit Cards option to select the credit card(s) you want to accept for order processing, with these further options:

  - Choose New to select to use a credit card not currently on the list, type in the card name (e.g., Novus, Diners Club), and click to check Make This Credit Card Available for Use Online. Next, select the data under Web Page Information you want to make customers provide when choosing this credit card for payment (card number, cardholder name, expiration date, and issuing bank) and/or click the Add/Remove button to modify selections under the Data Field Manager.

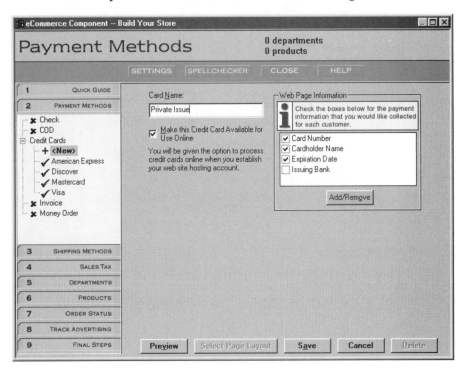

○ Select American Express to accept American Express credit cards and then check Make This Credit Card Available for Use Online. Next, select the data under Web Page Information that you want customers to provide when choosing this credit card for payment, and/or click the Add/Remove button to modify selections under the Data Field Manager.

○ Select Discover to accept Discover credit cards, and then follow the instructions for American Express above.

○ Select MasterCard to accept MasterCard, and then follow the instructions for American Express above.

○ Select Visa to accept Visa credit cards, and then follow the instructions for American Express above.

○ Choosing Invoice can amount to deferred payment, since you must generate a customer invoice for each item ordered. (Note that this is not something WebSite Complete provides for you; if you choose this option, you'll need to supply an invoice and handle payments.)

❖ Enabling the Money Order option allows customers to pay by money order sent to you before the order is shipped to them. Also click to select Make Money Orders Available for Online Use, check (if desired) to add an additional fee for accepting money orders and give the fee amount (flat or percentage), and click under Web Page Information if you want the number of the money order being used to pay for the order.

Step 3: Shipping Methods

Using the Shipping Methods option, you set the shipping options that your customers can select when they place their order on your site. As with the Payment Methods step, you'll see a tree of available options on the left side of the screen under Shipping Methods. From these options, click on entries to choose and then configure for use.

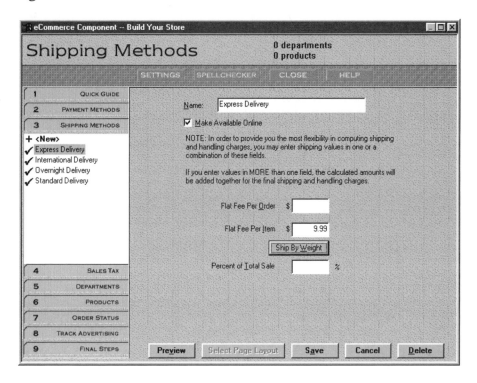

Tip

You may want to add higher fees for each "faster" level of delivery you offer to help offset your shipping and handling expenses, as well as to discourage customers from requesting that every order be expedited.

These shipping options include the following:

◆ Choose New to set up a form of delivery other than those listed. Then type the name of the delivery method under Name, click to check Make This Shipping Method Available for Use Online, and then type in the fee for this delivery: flat fee per order in dollars, flat fee per item in dollars, or percentage of total sale (you can use more than one fee and the total of the values will be added to the final cost of the order).

◆ Choose Express Delivery to establish this as a shipping method. Click to check Make Available Online and then type in the value(s) for the fee for this delivery: flat fee per order in dollars, flat fee per item in dollars, or percentage of total sale (you can use more than one fee and the total of the values will be added to the final cost of the order).

◆ Choose International Delivery to establish this as a shipping option and then follow the instructions under Express Delivery.

◆ Choose Overnight Delivery to establish this as a shipping option and then follow the instructions under Express Delivery.

◆ Choose Standard Delivery to establish this as a shipping option and then follow the instructions under Express Delivery.

Additionally, you can click the Ship by Weight button to open the Shipping Cost (Weight) screen to set specific weights and charges, as shown in the following graphic.

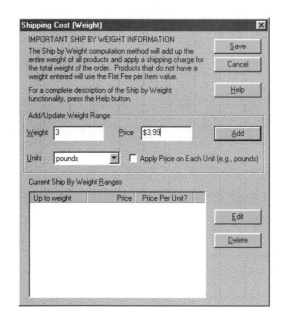

Warning

Standard Delivery should always be provided as an option, except in rare cases where a perishable product may be damaged unless its delivery is expedited; Overnight or Express should then be selected.

Tip

Check the Help menu under Shipping in WebSite Complete for information from Go Daddy on checking the shipping weight calculations from deliverers such as the U. S. Postal Service, UPS, and FedEx.

Step 4: Sales Tax

This step sets up information about any necessary sales tax specific to where you're doing business. Click the Sales Tax step button to configure information about how much sales tax to charge with orders. Once you click, you'll see a New item appear in the tree directly beneath the Sales Tax button.

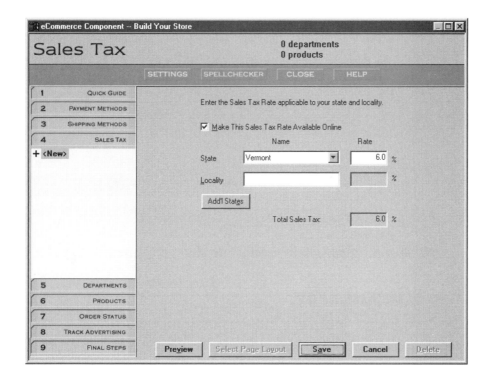

Then follow these steps:

1. Click the New entry.

2. Click to check Make This Sales Tax Rate Available Online (if not already checked).

3. In the row marked State, provide the following information:

◆ Under the Name column, click the drop-down list box and select the name of the state for which to apply sales tax.

◆ Under the Rate column, type in the tax rate for that state.

Tip

Unsure of sales tax rates for your area? Often, you can find this online through your state government's official Web site. You can also try other sites, such as The Sales Tax Clearinghouse at `http://thestc.com/STRates.stm`.

4. In the row marked Locality, provide this information if applicable:

◆ Type the name of the locality for which you're collecting sales tax (e.g., City of New York) in addition to the state sales tax you enter in step 3.

◆ Under the Rate column, type in the tax rate for that locality.

5. If you don't see a state listed, click the Add'l States button, enter the name of the new tax entity in the pop-up dialog box, and click OK. (If you need to add more, click the Add'l States button and click OK again to close.)

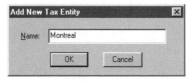

6. Repeat steps 1–4 for each state in which you need to collect sales tax.

Step 5: Departments

The Departments option helps to organize a multiproduct online store. Click this step button to establish departments for your online store in which specific categories of products may be listed. If you're running an online PC hardware store, for example, you might divide your 40 different products into departments such as "complete systems," "monitors," and "printers."

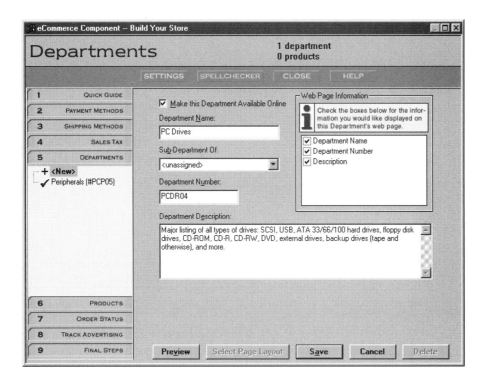

To establish departments, follow these steps after selecting Departments:

1. Click the New entry under Departments on the left side of the screen.

2. Click to check Make This Department Available Online (if not already checked).

3. Under Department Name, type in the name of the department you want to create.

4. Under Subdepartment Of, select nothing unless you need to create sub-departments to organize a large number of products.

5. Under Department Number, type in the number you want to assign to this department. This is a number of your own choosing and design (e.g., 1 or 015).

6. Under Department Description, type in information about the products to be found within this department.

7. On the right side of the screen, under Web Page Information, click to select any (or all) of the information that you want customers to provide (department name, department number, description).

8. Click Save (at the bottom of the window) to save this department entry.

9. Repeat Steps 1–8 to create additional departments.

Step 6: Products

Click this step button to add products to your online store. Once you click, you'll see a New entry pop up below the Products button.

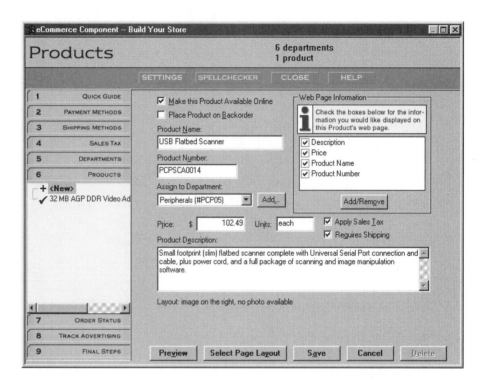

Follow these steps to add products to your online store:

1. Click the New entry.

2. Click to check Make This Product Available Online (if not already checked).

3. Check the box next to Place Products on Backorder only if the product is on backorder and you wish to note it here.

4. Under Product Name, type the name of the product you're adding as you want it to appear for customers.

5. Under Product Number, type the number you want to use as a unique identifying number for this item.

6. Under Assign to Department (if you've established departments), click the drop-down list box to choose a department for this product or click Add to add a new department in which to place it.

7. On the next line, type in the price in dollars, verify the Units entry (should be "each" unless you modify it), and then check Apply Sales Tax (if applicable) and/or Requires Shipping (if applicable).

8. Under Product Description, type in a short—but well-worded and informative—description of the product.

9. Click the Select Page Layout button at the bottom of the screen and select from the following:

◇ In the Step 1 field, click to select the layout you want to use for this product; if applicable, check the box to use this layout as the default product layout.

◇ In the Step 2 field, you can add an image. Click the Change button to bring up the Select an Image window, and then choose Browse to select the photo of your product you want to use or use available art from Select an Image. (You should already have these photos of your product stored in a separate folder on your hard drive. If you don't have images yet, skip this part of the step now and then come back to the Products section later and follow these steps to add an image.)

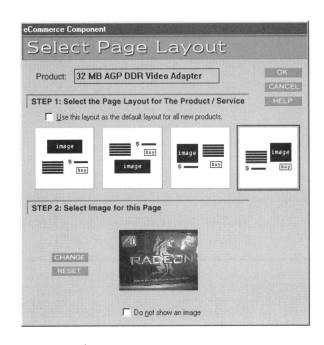

The image should then be displayed in preview format on the page, as seen in the image below.

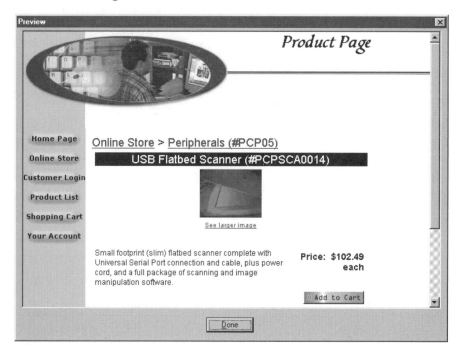

Click OK.

10. On the right side of the window, under Web Page Information, click to select any of the following you want to appear on the Web page for this product: description, price, product name, product number.

11. Click Save (bottom of window).

12. Repeat Steps 1–11 for each product you want to add to your online store.

Tip

If you have a lot of little stuff, taking up a Web page for each item could tax the amount of storage you have available for your site. Another option you can use is to create a page within WebSite Complete listing several items (along with photos) and adding a link at the bottom that takes customers to the Order Page (a page template you can select). Setting up this option works a lot like the process above, but it's quicker because you don't have to figure out departments and the like.

Note

For more information on digital photography, check out *Digital Photography! I Didn't Know You Could Do That...* by Erica Sadun (Sybex, 2000).

Digital Photography, Web Cams, and Your Online Store

Never underestimate the power of a good product image in potential sales.

Online marketing statistics indicate that customers are resistant to purchasing a product online if they don't have a good idea of what the product looks like (even if a detailed product description spells this out). And a bad image of a product is almost worse than no image at all, because a customer may find this more frustrating.

Even if you get artwork from distributors or product makers that you have permission to use in the product page of your online store, you may want to create your own images. Purchase a decent digital camera that can take a clear, crisp picture in a small format (since you want to avoid overly large images on your site).

Using a digital camera for this purpose is different than using a Web cam. A Web cam is usually used to take moving images for a live display on a Web site or to provide video in online video conferencing. Therefore, a Web cam may not be able to focus in on the fine detail needed to take product images.

The advantages of a digital camera are many:

◆ You don't harm the environment with all the chemicals involved in processing photos from traditional film (although you can go through a lot of batteries for the camera).

◆ You don't pay for film processing, because you just download the images from your camera directly into your PC using a cable connection.

◆ You save the time it would take to have photos developed, scan those photos into your PC, and edit them to the right look and the correct size.

If you think of digital photography as fuzzy, you probably remember the older, first- and second-generation digital cameras that often gave you a very grainy, indistinct image (even if you paid upwards of $500 for a model from top camera makers). Today's cameras can get close to 35mm-camera quality for under $400. The fancy models now come in 2- and 3-megapixel (million-pixel) formats, but a great camera for taking an 8"x 10" glossy is not necessarily the best camera for taking the small format Web site images you'll need.

Many cameras in the $250–400 range—including the Epson Photo PC series, the Agfa ePhoto series, and the Kodak DC200 (and later) series—are available in that price range and should allow you to take product images that can be used with very little extra effort.

To learn more about digital images and how to select a digital camera, check online technical references sites such as CNET™ at www.cnet.com and ZDNet™ at www.zdnet.com for online guides to digital camera features and shopping.

Step 7: Order Status

Click this step button to configure options for notifying customers that their order has been received for processing and/or has shipped.

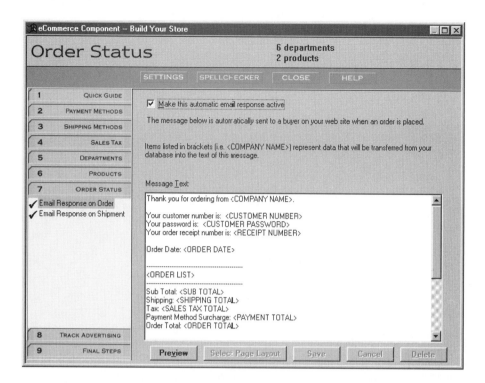

When you select this step, you'll see that two options appear on the left side:

- ◇ Click E-Mail Response on Order to display the template sent via e-mail to the customer as confirmation that the order has been received.

- ◇ Click E-Mail Response on Shipment to display the template sent via e-mail to the customer as confirmation that the order has been shipped.

Choose one to open the template in the main window.

The information in <brackets> is automatically supplied by Go Daddy's servers and includes items like your company name, customer number, order number, and others. However, if you want to customize other parts of the text, you can click the part of text you want to change and just begin typing. If you do modify the text, make sure to save those changes to the e-mail template.

Step 8: Track Advertising

The Track Advertising step configures your site for tracking specific ads. This is an optional feature you can implement if you advertise in more than one place (either online or offline). When a customer arrives and places an order on your e-commerce site, they can also tell you where they heard about your site by choosing from a list of options. The customer's response is then tallied in your site statistics and managed by Go Daddy's servers as they handle your other details so that you can then determine where new visitors are coming from and which avenues of promotion or advertising are working best for you.

When you choose to use this feature, you'll be prompted to establish an advertising source code for each type of advertising you want to track. That sounds complicated, but it's just some unique identifying code you create yourself to separate one ad effort from another.

For example, say you decide to have four specific avenues of advertising promotion when you first start your e-commerce site (more on promotion efforts in the next chapter). These include an ad in *The Collector's Quarterly* in July (7/01) and again in October (10/01), an ad in *The Clarion News*, and a banner ad running on a network called Link Exchange. Since you need to uniquely identify each, you could set the following source codes for each ad: TCQ0701, TCQ1001, TCN, and LE.

To track these codes in WebSite Complete, perform the following steps:

1. Open your Web project in WebSite Complete and click the Build Online Store button on the toolbar.

2. Click Track Advertising.

3. Next to Advertising Source Code, type **TCQ1001** to track your October 1st, 2001, ad in *The Collector's Quarterly*.

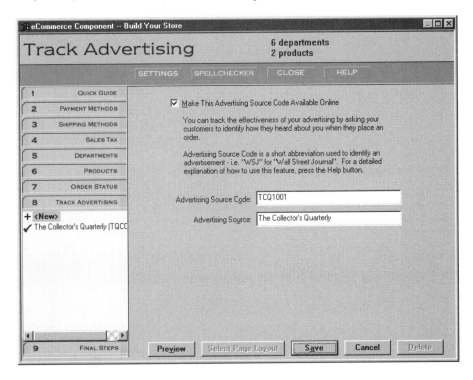

4. Next to Advertising Source, type **The Collector's Quarterly**.

5. Click Save.

6. Repeat for the remaining ads.

Step 9: Final Steps

This step button takes you through the last four steps necessary to be sure your online store is ready to be uploaded to Go Daddy servers, processed, and organized into the full online store visitors will see. As with plug-ins, you don't see the fully prepared online store until it's available on the Web.

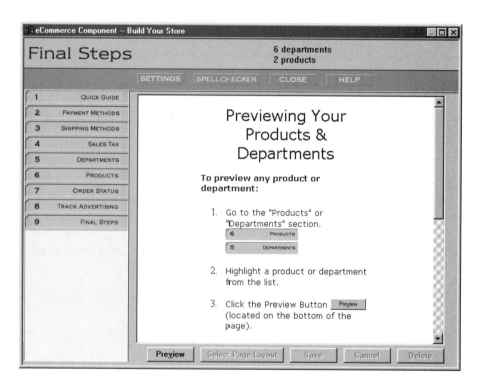

These final steps include the following:

1. Click Review the E-Commerce Checklist to go through a checklist of components covered here.

2. Click Preview Your Departments and Products Pages to preview your product pages individually, as well as to view departments.

3. Click Spell-Check Your E-Commerce data to remind you to click the Spell Checker button above to verify spelling throughout your online store (don't forget!).

4. Click Close the E-Commerce Window and Return to Your Project to remind you to click Close to quit building your store and return to your Web project to prepare to publish (if desired).

Publishing Your Online Store

Now you're ready to publish your data and put Go Daddy's servers to work assembling that data into an online store. Depending on the size of your store, the number of products you offer, and the number of product images, this publishing session may take substantially longer than your first one did in chapters 4–6. Be patient, especially if you have a slow Internet connection.

Follow these steps to publish:

1. Review your changes, spell-check, and close the E-Commerce Component window, if you haven't already done so.

2. From the main WebSite Complete window, click the Final Steps tab.

3. Click the Start button in the Publish Your Web to the Internet section.

   You'll be prompted to connect to the Internet. As noted in previous chapters, you may need to connect through your usual means (AOL software, dial-up networking connection, etc.) first and then click this button.

4. If you've already set up both your Web hosting and merchant account with WebSite Complete, you will be prompted to provide your username and password to publish.

   If you've set up a hosting account, but not your merchant account, provide your username and password and then click Online Manager to apply for your merchant account.

Your online store will then be published to your Internet Web site. If your merchant account is already in place, people can begin using your site immediately to make online purchases and pay by credit card. If you apply for your merchant account at the time of publishing, you won't be able to process credit cards online until your merchant account application is approved (about a week). If your merchant account is declined, you will still be able to accept checks, money orders, and CODs, as you wish.

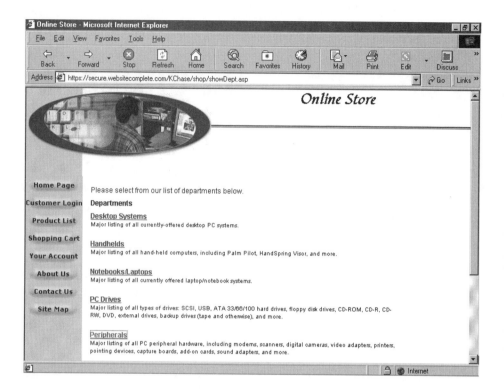

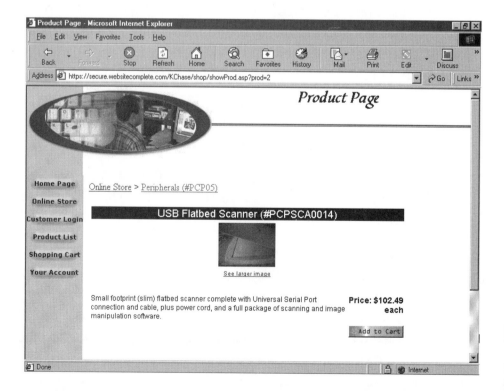

Using Online Manager to Manage Your Site and Your Store

Online Manager is Go Daddy's interface for allowing you to access information about your hosting account and your online store. It's responsible for tracking all information about the orders placed in your online store and about your overall site.

The following options and data are available to you under Online Manager:

- basic information about your account

- basic Web site statistics for your site

- access reports that indicate sales activity on your e-commerce site by order, by product, by sales, tax, and more

- a method to look up customer information and modify customer records (for change of address, phone number, etc.)

- a method to process customer orders for shipment

- refund orders

Follow these steps to access Online Manager:

1. Connect to the Internet using your usual connection.

2. Load your Web browser.

3. In the browser's address window, type in the URL sent to you via e-mail when you set up your account with Go Daddy.

   Or, you can also go to the Go Daddy site, log in, and choose Online Manager.

4. When prompted, provide your username and password.

189

Chapter 10

Promoting Your E-Commerce Web Site

One perhaps sad truth about Web commerce is that you can spend all the time you like designing and creating a dynamic, good-looking, and perfectly working Web site, but unless you promote the site, almost no one will see it. There are many sites out there: More than 30 million domains have been registered, and most of these have at least some fledgling Web site attached to them. More than 10 million of these are estimated to conduct some form of e-commerce—either directly through products or services offered by small businesses and Web-based entrepreneurs or indirectly as affiliates of mega-commerce sites.

Using search words and registering your site with large Web search engines can help your site be found in a search, but you should realize that it may be one of possibly thousands of entries that come up in the same search. Thus, you need to think about ways you can promote your site to attract more potential customers to see what you have to offer.

Getting to Know Your Audience

Before you make any plans for promoting your Web site, you need to stop and think about your intended audience. Some e-commerce sites, by nature of either the products offered or the expansion plans of the entrepreneur, lend themselves to very global promotion. For example, if you're selling antiques, videotapes, hard candies, or vacation property, you may want to go far beyond your local city or state to attract customers to your products or services. But if you're a local pastry shop, restaurant, dentist, or insurance agent, your focus may be on promoting your products and services within a specific geographic area.

Also, some professionals may establish e-commerce sites more to appeal to other professionals in related fields. For example, some sites may only sell wholesale to other dealers in medical supply, home decorating, or consumer goods. Thus, some of the promotion venues mentioned in this chapter will apply more to a global promotion, and some will apply to a localized promotion.

Exploring the Avenues of E-Commerce Promotion

In this section, you'll learn about the various avenues available to you for promoting your e-commerce Web site. In choosing your promotional methods, be sure to keep your target audience in mind, and don't forget to weigh the costs against the potential gain in clientele. Some methods will involve relatively little or no cost beyond your labor, and others—such as massive Web banner and print advertising—can become quite expensive.

Promoting with Printed Material

Most likely, you already promote your business phone number in all your printed material so that customers or clients can reach you. You should also include the address for your e-commerce site in anything you now do—from correspondence to advertising to promotional printings.

Many newspapers and chambers of commerce, for example, now have online community bulletin boards serving their local area. They may also have printed supplements to their papers or brochures that include local business sites. Some allow local businesses to post a basic Web address to something like an online community board maintained on a Web site devoted to an overall view of the town, city, or county. Check to see what may be available in your area and how you may be able to use such a venue to advertise your site for more localized business.

Note

Web site addresses are usually printed on promotional materials as simply "www. *yourdomain*.com," not as "http://www.*yourdomain*.com."

Do *You* Send Out Press Releases?

Some stores and businesses send out press releases to local newspapers, trade journals, and consumer magazines whenever they launch a new product or product line, become the exclusive distributors of a potentially hot new product, or otherwise "make news."

If you do this—or feel inclined to do this—don't forget to include your Web site address in your press release. You can direct readers to your Web site as well as provide your phone number if they want more information on what you offer and who you are.

This list includes some of the printed items to which you can add your Web site address:

- ◆ business stationery, letterheads, logos, and business cards
- ◆ packing materials and shipping labels
- ◆ catalogs and special mailings
- ◆ promotional t-shirts and other give-away products such as bumper stickers, matchbooks, postcards, calendars, bookmarks, pens, pencils, and mouse pads
- ◆ outdoor business signs
- ◆ print ads and special marketing vehicles (such as a local store that advertises its URL on a local diner's placemat)

- magnetic display signs for a company vehicle
- flyers and brochures
- in-store and window display banners
- menus

Using Other Media Advertising

Many small businesses and companies use media advertising other than print ads, such as radio ads or low-cost spots on their local cable television feeds.

If you use these, don't forget to mention the name of your Web site in the ad. This is one time when a short, easy-to-remember domain name is a distinct advantage. A long or complicated name is easily forgotten, even in the short time that it takes to walk to a computer and type the name into the browser address window.

Promoting via E-Mail

There's a great deal of divergent opinion on how effective e-mail advertising actually is. Many users will delete such e-mail faster than they throw regular junk mail in the wastebasket. Others may visit your site, but not to order products. (They may instead want to find a way to contact you to tell you how much they don't appreciate your unsolicited advertising in their mailbox!) In fact, some statistics suggest that very few actual new customers are gained through this method.

If you've been using e-mail for any period of time, you are already aware that your mailbox can be flooded by far more **spam** than real correspondence. You—and each user who gets spam—must deal with the inconvenience and potentially pay higher connection fees through your Internet provider for having to handle it. Also, mail servers around the world have difficulty keeping up with the volume.

spam
unsolicited e-mail advertising

On the other hand, when entrepreneurs or small business owners set up an e-commerce site for the first time, they may feel that sending out an e-mail blitz to several thousand people they don't know is a good way to attract business to their site. (As a friend who admits to being a serious self-promoter once told me, "It's only spam if somebody *else* sends it.") Indeed, your mailbox is apt to be full of spam from companies offering you directed marketing lists of e-mail addresses that you can buy and use to do a mass mailing. These groups often target newly registered domain owners like you, hoping you'll buy their lists to promote your site.

Instead, you may want to consider trying a different way of promoting in e-mail. For example, you can create your own electronic newsletter of tips, in-store specials, special service packages, and featured products, and then send it via e-mail to those who request it through a link on your Web site. If you have a physical store or office, you can provide a newsletter sign-up sheet for your customers and clients who stop by. If you take orders by phone, you can let customers know about this newsletter and give them the option of being included in your e-mail distribution list.

You can use various methods to set up an electronic newsletter. Electronic newsletters can be in plain text with working links to specific pages on your e-commerce site, or they can be done in HTML so that you can apply colors, fancy formatting, and images to the body of the newsletter. Many Web-development sites offer HTML code that you can add to your site to set this up, and some offer add-on applets you can install to handle this for you.

Exploring Web-Based Advertising and Promotion

There are many ways you can promote your site through online, Web-based vehicles. You'll want to explore as many of them as seem feasible to you in getting your Web site address in front of as many potential shoppers or clients as possible.

Some of the methods in this section involve buying Web ad space, while others require you to contact other vendors or individuals running sites similar or complementary to yours so that you can cross-promote sites.

> **Tip**
>
> Here's an easy, no-cost promotion: Include text in your Web site advising visitors how to add your site to their Favorites list (if they use Internet Explorer) or bookmark the site (if they use Netscape), so they can easily return. You can also recommend that they let friends and associates know about you.

Promoting with Banner Network Ads

banner network ads
also called banner ads, these ads usually appear at the top or bottom of a Web site's main page and, when clicked, link a user to the site of the company whose ad is running

Buying Web ad space is much less expensive than traditional print ads. Many companies offer special ways to promote a Web site through the use of **banner network ads** placed on other sites. The best known of these—and one you may hear mentioned often—is one formerly known as Link Exchange®.

Link Exchange was formerly a free advertising contingent where you simply had to add HTML code to your Web page to provide a banner network ad for them; in turn, they listed your site on other sites.

Link Exchange, however, has since been purchased by Microsoft and rolled into their Microsoft bCentral™ small business services site at `http://store/bcentral/ledefault.asp`. The bCentral site itself is worth visiting at `http://bCentral.com/default.asp` because it offers articles and tips on promoting and developing a small business, including the use of a company Web site to do this.

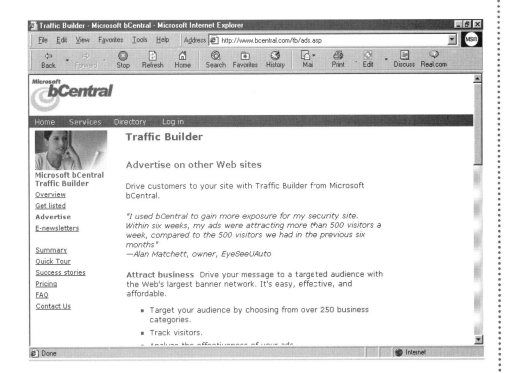

Also, Link Exchange is no longer free and is now rolled into something called Traffic Builder: It sells banner network advertising by number of **ad views**. The cost of these ads and Traffic Builder membership varies, so you should check their sign-up site at `http://trafficbuilder.bcentral.com/system/tbchoice.cfm` for current details. Just in the weeks this book was being written, the structure and pricing appeared to change about three times.

One advantage with using this type of network is its overall size. It has more than 450,000 participating member sites, giving a broad range of different types of sites where an ad might appear. Link Exchange boasts statistics from industry analysis firms stating that their ads reach almost 70 percent of all Web users. And you can target ads by choosing to advertise within one of the more than 250 categories of sites the former Link Exchange Banner Network reaches.

Using Professional Referral

If you belong to a professional association or a business development group that runs a Web site, you should check to see if it permits the listing of member sites. This type of referral can be another good way of getting additional visitors to your site. Also, many visitors may feel more confident in buying a product or service from your site if they see you listed in a professional directory of members.

ad views

refers to the number of times an ad is displayed on sites within that advertising network; ads usually change each time a Web visitor reloads or revisits a Web site with such advertising

Trading Link Promotion with Others

If you know other vendors or professionals in your field, or in directly complementary fields, who also run professional or e-commerce sites, you may want to offer to provide each other with complimentary links to your respective sites. Cross-promotion helps if, for example, someone shopping on another site wants to see a bigger selection or locate products or services they couldn't locate on the first site. They then see your site listed and may come over to visit.

Exploring Web Rings

Web rings
groups of Web sites that are tied together by some common theme, message, or content (including e-commerce in general and various types of online sales specifically)

Web rings are created on a special type of Web server, called a ring server, and link to other Web sites within the ring. The theory here is that if a Web site visitor looking for particular information or a particular product happens upon one site in the Web ring, they can easily move to similar sites in the same ring, offering more potential exposure for all.

Many different types of Web rings exist, covering such topics as graphics and Web site development, medical information, collections of digital sound files, and different types of stores. Also, many different groups run their own organized forms of Web rings. If you're interested in exploring this option for cross-promotions, just search through one of the Web search engines such as Yahoo!® or Google© to find lists of them, like the Yahoo! WebRing group at www.webring.com.

Using Search Engines

In Chapter 6, "Publishing Your E-Commerce Web Site," you took the final steps to prepare your first e-commerce site for publishing. You added both a description of your site and search words to help identify you to Web search engines such as Yahoo!, AltaVista®, Excite™, and Google.

Now that your site has been published, it should not remain static. As you choose to build the online component of your company or service, you may add or remove products, articles, seasonal material, and so on. Those changes should be then reflected in your search words.

Check your Web site's search words on a regular basis, and try to update your search words every time you revise your site. This is one more small detail that can make a difference in the traffic on your site, and it differentiates you from the entrepreneurs who take a more lackadaisical approach to defining their Web-based business.

Beware of Offers to Market Your Site

If you've been using e-mail for some time, you've likely received more than your share of unsolicited advertising hawking almost every kind of product or service. One popular blitz is an offer by various marketing companies to register you with hundreds, if not thousands, of Web search engines for some nominal (or even not so nominal) fee.

All too often, however, these firms are just offering to do work you can pretty easily do yourself, both through WebSite Complete and on your own. Even worse, they purport to help get you noticed by large search engines that will very likely pick up your site on their own. Large Web search companies use techniques to scan the Web for new sites and categorize them according to search words both applied and even some not supplied. However, your chances of being included increase if you apply for inclusion.

While someone who wants to actively promote their e-commerce site may not want to risk delay or possible miscategorization by waiting for a Web search engine to include them, they should also think carefully before paying money to another company to do the work for them.

Registering with Search Engines in WebSite Complete

WebSite Complete includes a way to access its online wizard and help you register your e-commerce site with several of the major Web search engines for free.

The one exception to this, however, is the Yahoo! search engine. Because Yahoo! is not a search engine in the traditional sense of the word, but an organized directory of Web-based businesses and resources, there is a some-what more complicated registration process that may take substantially longer to complete. Thus, if you want to register with Yahoo!, you can do it yourself by visiting their site and clicking their How to Suggest a Site link or by typing this address into your browser's address window: `http://docs.yahoo.com/info/suggest`.

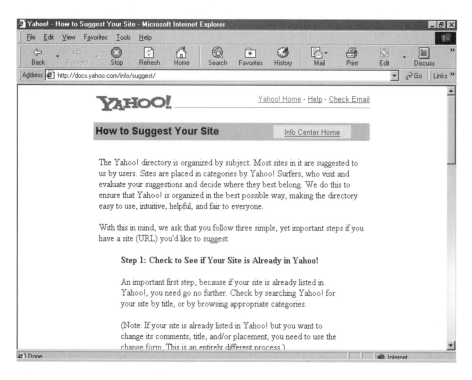

To use WebSite Complete's easy wizard for registering with major Web search engines, follow these steps:

1. With WebSite Complete open to your Web site project, click the Final Steps tab in Control Panel.

2. Click Start in the Register with Internet Search Engines box.

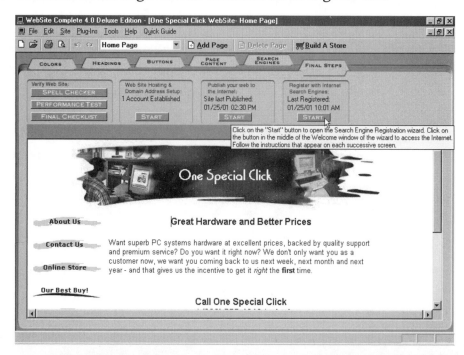

3. On the Search Engine Registration screen, click to select the search engines with which you want to register. Click Continue.

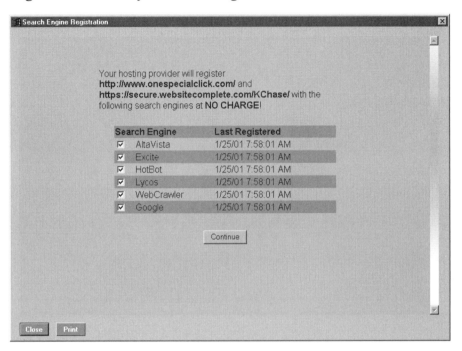

Registering with other Web Search Engines

Not all Web search engines are listed in WebSite Complete's registration wizard for a couple of reasons. One reason is that Web search companies tend to combine with each other often and change names. For example, Snap.com was bought by the National Broadcasting Company (NBC) and has been changed and combined into NBCi.com. Other reasons are that new ones debut and different search engines go in and out of cyber fashion constantly. Everyone's favorite search engine this week may change next week.

If you find a Web search engine that's not on the list to which you'd like to register, visit that search site and look for a link related to this. Some sites call it Register Your Site, while others may call it something like Recommend a Good Site. Follow the directions provided to either recommend or directly submit your e-commerce site for inclusion.

Tip

Some sites offer a small discount or a one-time flat fee of a few dollars—or even a free product—to customers if they refer someone who actually places an order on the site.

Chapter 11

Maintaining and Managing Your E-Commerce Web Site

Your e-commerce site has been designed, published, tested, and revised, and an online store has been added. Now your next role begins: site manager keeping your Web site well maintained and the e-commerce side of it well managed.

This final chapter takes you through the elements you need to consider in keeping your site fresh and up-to-date. It also explains the tools available for managing your site; some apply to a general business site, while other tools are specifically for e-commerce.

Maintaining Your E-Commerce Site

Web sites that look like they receive little or no attention once they are posted tend to get very little repeat traffic from visitors. If visitors feel that nothing is apt to be updated, why should they bother going back?

While this doesn't mean that you need to be a slave to your e-commerce site, you do want to check it over regularly and note any content (text, links, products, and so on) that needs to be modified or removed. You should perform these actions at least every few weeks, as needed, using the addition, deletion, and modification techniques from Chapter 4, "Building Your First E-Commerce Web Site," and Chapter 5, "Adding Special Features to Your E-Commerce Web Site." Also review online store specifics and related common operations covered in Chapter 9, "Building Your Online Store."

As you look through your site, be on the watch for such problems as the following:

- ◆ Remove any expired seasonal material. For example, many well-maintained e-commerce sites promptly remove all December holiday artwork, promotions, and text by January 2.

- ◆ Where possible, avoid placing visible dates in any text or pages that are not updated regularly.

- ◆ Modify any pages that need updating (for example, a January "specials" list still appearing in March).

- ◆ Remove any pages that are no longer needed or desired.

- ◆ Delete any links to other sites or pages that are no longer available.

- ◆ Use the Event Calendar Manager to remove outdated entries and old events listed in the event calendar.

- ◆ For products that are temporarily out of stock, change the product's status online to let the customer know if a product is on backorder before they place their order.

- ◆ Remove products you no longer carry.

- ◆ Modify the price under each product on the product page when there are price changes.

- Delete departments you no longer feature.

- Change any products and/or images you want to change.

- It's also good to check that photos are where they're supposed to be and displayed properly. If a photo or image is not showing properly for you locally, it won't after you publish it or when customers visit your site.

You should also look at your site to determine if any features or anything else is missing. If so, you can either place this feature or features on your "pending" site for your Web site (discussed in Chapter 3, "Planning Your First E-Commerce Site") or make the addition when you make these other changes.

Using Newsletters and Columns for Site Content

An expert's column or newsletter can be a good professional addition to a Web site. With an e-commerce or service-oriented site, such a newsletter or column can be used to call particular attention to one or more products or services.

For example, someone selling stationery supplies in an online store might use a newsletter to highlight back-to-school products before September. Another site selling computer software might add a column discussing how users can protect themselves against computer viruses, with links to antivirus software products they carry.

But if you decide to employ this feature, be sure you update it regularly. Many site creators start such a feature and then lose interest after a few weeks or months. Don't place an exact date on a newsletter or column if it will sit there for many months.

Thus, try to set an attainable goal for updating. If the newsletter or column will be changed only a few times a year and you feel compelled to date it somehow, you can call it the "Quarterly Newsletter" or "Our Winter Feature" (and update it seasonally).

Finally, beware of any claims you make in a feature like this, especially if you're thinking about publishing derogatory statements about a competing product. Government agencies, like the Federal Trade Commission, and the courts have started looking more closely at the claims that e-commerce sites make.

Keeping Products Updated

This section provides step-by-step instructions on how to perform important product-related modifications to keep your site fully updated, including how to place products on backorder, how to remove products completely, or how to make them temporarily unavailable.

Placing Products on Backorder

Customers get frustrated—and have been known to write or call with angry complaints—when they complete the ordering process only to discover then that the product is on backorder. Thus, whenever you have a situation where you're temporarily out of stock on a product that you expect in the reasonable future, it's best to modify the product description to reflect this change in status.

Here's how to modify a product's status:

1. With WebSite Complete open to your Web project, click the Plug-Ins option on the menu bar and select E-Commerce.

2. From the E-Commerce Component window, click to select the Products step button on the left side of the screen.

3. Locate the product you want to modify in the list below the Products button and click to open that product's information in the main window.

4. Click to check the Place Product on Backorder option.

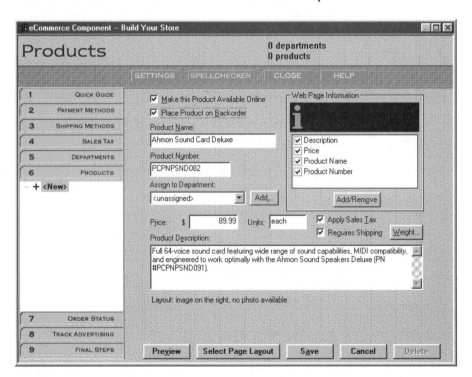

5. Click Save.

Tip

If you're unsure of the future availability of the product and want to avoid customers requesting backorders you may be unable to fulfill, you may want to uncheck the Make This Product Available Online option detailed later in this section.

Removing Products from Your Online Store

If you no longer carry a product, the product should be removed from your online store.

To accomplish this, follow these steps:

1. With WebSite Complete open to your Web project, click the Plug-Ins option on the menu bar and select E-Commerce.

2. From the E-Commerce Component window, click to select the Products step button on the left side of the screen.

3. Locate the product you want to delete in the list below the Products button and click to open that product's information in the main window.

4. Click the Delete button at the bottom of the screen.

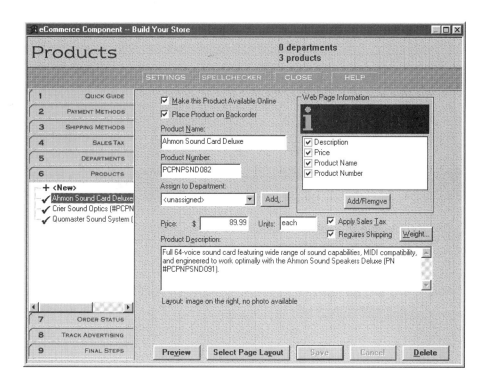

5. When prompted, confirm the deletion by clicking Yes.

6. Repeat for any other products you wish to remove.

Making a Product Unavailable for Viewing

You can remove a product from a listing that the customer sees on your site without deleting the product record itself.

Follow these steps to do this:

1. With WebSite Complete open to your Web project, click the Plug-Ins option on the menu bar and select E-Commerce.

2. From the E-Commerce Component window, click to select the Products step button on the left side of the screen.

3. Locate the product you want to modify in the list below the Products button and click to open that product's information in the main window.

4. Click to uncheck the option labeled Make This Product Available Online.

5. Click Save.

Warning

Remember that you need to republish your site after making any modifications to have these changes reflected on your live Web site.

Managing Your E-Commerce Site

From building your online store in Chapter 9, you're aware of the need for using a merchant account. Remember that you use Online Manager, which is located on a secured part of Go Daddy's Web servers (and not from WebSite Complete), to apply for a merchant account or to activate your account.

But Online Manager does more: It's a sort of central control system for your Web site, as well as for your online store, and it allows you to both manage aspects of your store and check information about how you do business. This information includes the generation of sales reports, traffic statistics for your site, and the ability to modify a customer's record to note change of address, phone number, or other record data.

Using Online Manager Tools

The tools you'll need to manage your site and your online store via Online Manager can be reached from anywhere that you have an Internet connection and a Web browser. This means you can work from your home or office/business, or even if you're away on a trip.

To access the tools, follow these steps:

1. Connect to the Internet.

2. Launch your Web browser.

3. Type this address in your browser's address window, where *yourdomain*.com is the actual domain name of your site: **http://www.*yourdomain*.com/manager**.

   Click Enter.

4. From the login window, type in your full domain name in the format of **www.*yourdomain*.com**, then type your username and password.

   Click Login.

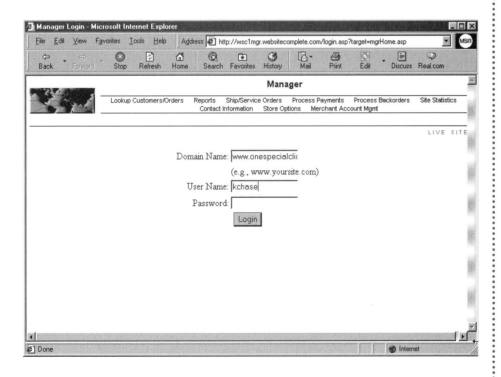

Online Manager then opens to a menu of manager options. Note that the same bulleted options here are reflected in a more textual window at the top of the page. You can click from either section to choose an option.

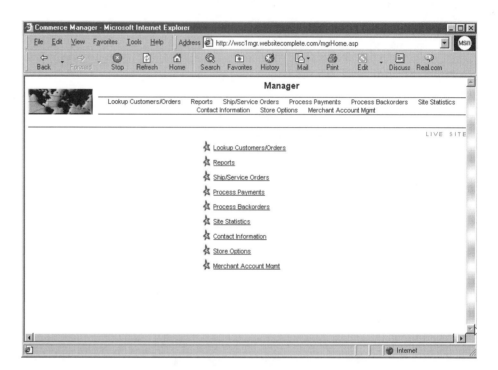

Warning

If you allow much time to elapse between performing various functions under Online Manager, you may be prompted to log in to Online Manager again. Consider this a security feature: If you step away from your desk for a prolonged period of time, it will be less likely someone unauthorized will come along and make or change entries for you.

Looking Up Customer Orders

Click the Look Up Customers/Orders option to find customer information (billing or shipping) by various criteria.

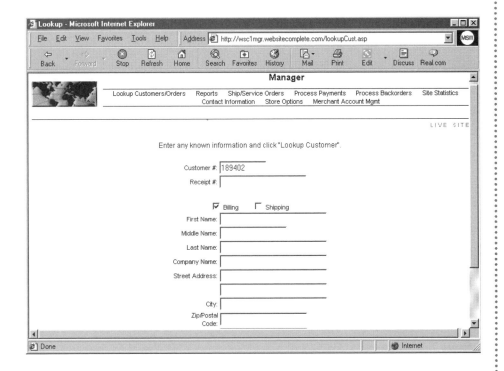

The criteria include the following:

- ◆ customer number
- ◆ receipt number
- ◆ name
- ◆ company name
- ◆ address

Note

The term "order number" is represented in Online Manager reports as "receipt number."

Generating Reports

Click the Reports option to open the reporting tool for your site. You can generate online reports about your Web sales, grouped by categories.

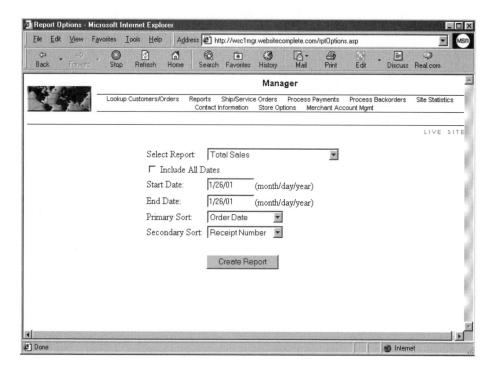

The following categories are available by clicking the drop-down list box next to the Select Report field:

- ◇ The Total Sales option establishes the total amount of business you've done.

- ◇ The Sales by Product option checks to see how well, or poorly, a specific product is doing on your site.

- ◇ Use the Sales by Advertising Source Code option to see which ads are the best and worst performers for generating new sales.

- ◇ Use the Refunds Processed option to establish where potential refund problems exist (bad product, for example).

- ◇ Choose the Sales Tax Due option to establish quickly how much you owe in collected sales tax.

- ◇ Click the Order Status option to see an analysis of your current orders and their processing status.

You can also choose to generate reports by specified dates. Click the appropriate check box if you want to generate a report that includes all dates, or provide the start date and end date of the period you want to analyze.

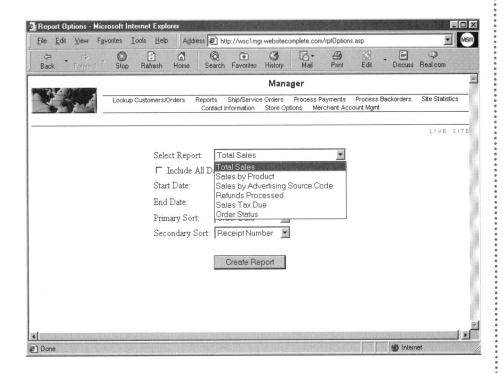

Finally, you can perform both a primary and a secondary sort on the information assembled for this report:

1. Click the drop-down list box next to the Primary Sort field.

2. Choose from the following sort options: Order Date, Receipt Number, Customer Number, Item Cost, Shipping Total, Tax Total, Misc Total, or Total Cost.

3. Repeat step 2 for secondary sort.

4. Click Create Report.

Shipping and Servicing Orders

Click the Ship/Service Orders option to see a report of all orders ready for shipment. This report includes these fields: Ship Item, Print Packing Slip, Date Ordered, Order Number, Customer Number, Customer Name, Item Number, Item Name, and Quantity.

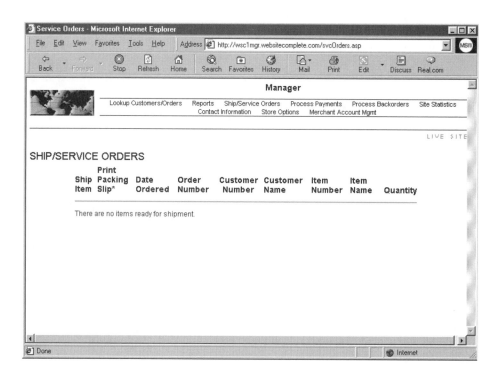

Processing Payments

Click the Process Payments option to see a list of recent payments—either pending or received (from credit card transactions, for example) or by detail (what was processed, total cost, payment type, order and customer number, authorization code, etc.).

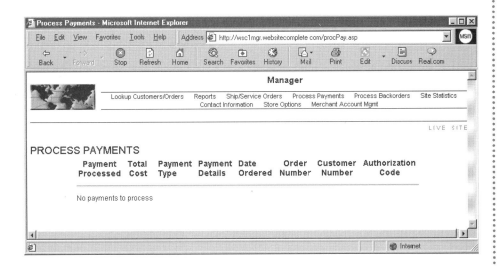

Processing Backorders

Click the Process Backorders option if you need to process any customer back-orders. For example, use this option if a customer orders a product that is not currently in stock and you accept the order pending receipt of new inventory.

Compiling Site Statistics

For **site statistics**, choose this option to see a graphical analysis of activity on your e-commerce Web site, as shown below.

site statistics
information about a site (who visited, where they were from, what pages they looked at, etc.) that can help you identify the level of traffic to your site and offers some indication of who your audience may be

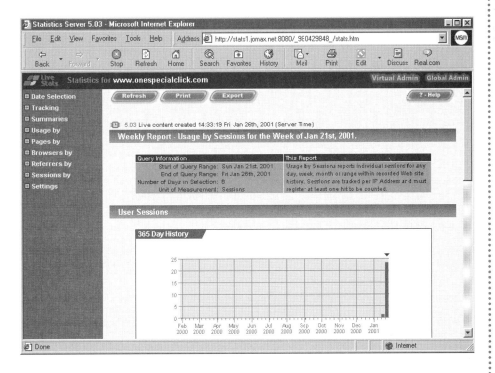

You'll see a graph displaying overall user activity on your site by month and year, representing a full 365 days (one year). Click the entries on the left under Live Stats to recompile this information by certain criteria, such as the following:

◆ Use Date Selection to choose a specific time period to review.

◆ Use Tracking to watch for specific information you want to track, such as where the traffic to your site is coming from.

◆ To use Summaries, click Yesterday, Last Week, or Last Month for a detailed summary of activity on your site, presented in text form.

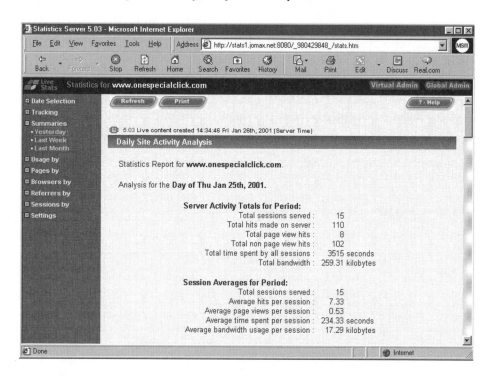

◆ Click Usage By to see details concerned with sessions, hits (how many times the site was accessed), session time (how long users spent on your site per session), and more.

◆ Click Pages By to see detailed information on activity and issues concerning specific pages on your site (for example, to see which are least often viewed, which pages draw a user's attention the longest, and more).

◆ Click Browsers By to see a summary of the various Internet browsers (and their different versions) being used by customers to access your site.

- ◆ Click Referrers By to see how your customers are finding you (referred by another site, by a search engine, etc.).

- ◆ Click Sessions By to see where your customers are coming from in terms of ISP, agency, or physical location.

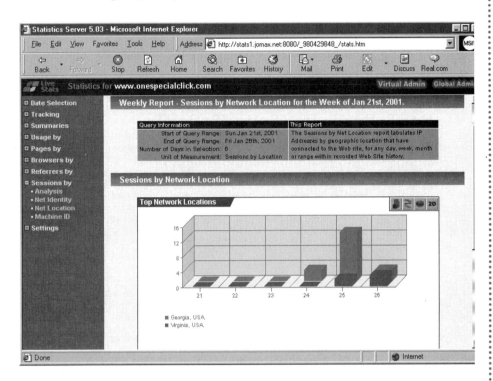

- ◆ Click Settings to set up the look and language of your statistics. (Note, however, that at the time of this writing, your only choice is Original English.)

Tip

If you want to print out a copy of any of the reports you see here, click the Print button in the upper-left part of your screen. Click Refresh to refresh the information as necessary.

Modifying Contact Information

Click the Contact Information option if you need to change any of the details about your Web site contact's name, address, phone number, or e-mail.

Setting Store Options

Click Store Options to set certain criteria for your online store.

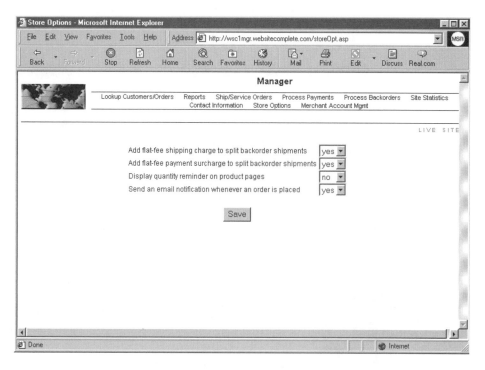

A menu will appear on the next page and give you four options. Use the drop-down box at the right to make your choice (Yes or No). These are your four options:

◆ Do you want to add a flat-fee shipping charge to split backorder shipments? Choose Yes to add a fee for shipping when you need to split an order into a part that ships now and another that ships when the back-ordered item(s) is back in stock.

◆ Do you want to add a flat-fee payment surcharge to split backorder shipments? Choose Yes to add a fee for the extra effort involved in processing a backorder.

◆ Do you want to display a quantity reminder on product pages? Choose Yes if you want to indicate to customers the limited quantity available (perhaps to encourage them to order now rather than later).

◆ Do you want to send an e-mail notification whenever an order is placed? Choose Yes if you want to provide this communication to customers (may save you a call or fax from customers wondering if you've received their online orders).

Click Save to save any changes you've made to settings.

Managing Your Merchant Account

With the Merchant Account Mgmt option, you can do one of two things. You can activate the merchant account you've already applied and been approved for (a number of merchant account types besides Go Daddy are listed here). Or you can sign up for a new merchant account.

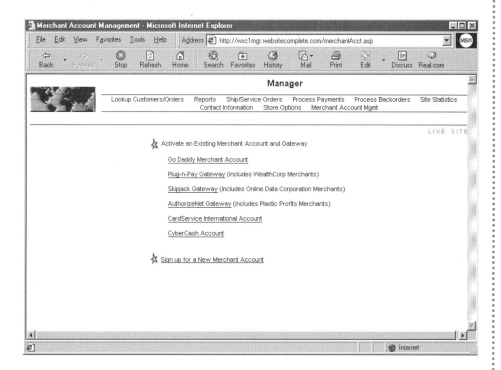

Congratulations! If you've reached this point, you've taken the basic steps necessary to set up your own professional Web site that may include an online store. Good luck with your venture.

But don't forget: Your responsibility as an effective Web designer and e-entrepreneur doesn't end when you first get the site looking and working right. Maintain, update, and continue to make your site as inviting as the best physical stores, and visit it often yourself to make certain everything is in proper order. The best sites do this, and you should, too.

Appendix

Help with Using WebSite Complete

This section is designed to help you work through difficulties you may experience using WebSite Complete. It also steps you through what you need to do to use WebSite Complete from two different computers (for example, from your home and your work PC) and how to uninstall WebSite Complete, if you need to do so.

Troubleshooting Questions on WebSite Complete

A major first step with any problem with Website Complete would be to go to www.godaddy.com and see if there are any new versions, patches, or downloads available that are not yet installed. This can save a lot of headaches as well as your precious time.

Question

Help! After a problem with my PC, I rebooted, and now I can't get WebSite Complete to load. I even tried restarting and trying again. Nothing! Have I lost my Web project?

Answer

First, bring up Task Manager by pressing Ctrl+Alt+Del once (twice or more restarts your machine) and see if WebSite Complete is listed as already running. If it is, select it in the list and click End Task. Then try again to launch WebSite Complete.

Explanation

If you can't get it to work, you can reinstall WebSite Complete on top of itself. Follow the instructions in Chapter 2, "Getting Started with WebSite Complete 4.0," for installing the software. The setup software will recognize that you already have WebSite Complete installed and let you know that it will overwrite that installation. Don't worry; your Web project should be safe (but remember to use the Backup feature).

If all else fails, you can try uninstalling the software first by going to Control Panel, double-clicking Add/Remove Programs, selecting WebSite Complete in the listing, and then clicking the Add/Remove button. Then reinstall it following the installation steps noted in Chapter 2.

Question

After I've been working in WebSite Complete for a bit of time, the software will sometimes lock up, forcing me to close it. Or the colors will distort as I move between screens. This happens more frequently when I have to go online through the software and then go back to WebSite Complete's main screen. What can I do?

Answer

Your system resources are chunks of working memory that Windows allocates for Desktop operations. Low system resources can, therefore, be one cause of this. Check your system resources the next time this happens by going to Control Panel, double-clicking the System icon, and choosing the Performance tab. As long as you have more than 30 percent (some systems can go as low as 10 or 15 percent) available, this shouldn't be a problem.

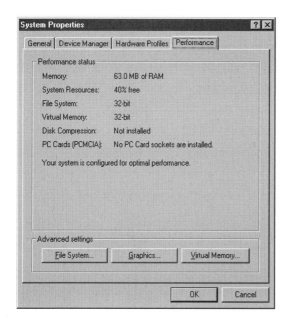

If you load lots of programs at Windows Startup, you could restrict the working memory you have available to you. From the Start button, click Run, type **MSCONFIG**, and then click OK. Choose the Startup tab, and click to uncheck any programs you don't absolutely have to have running every time Windows reloads.

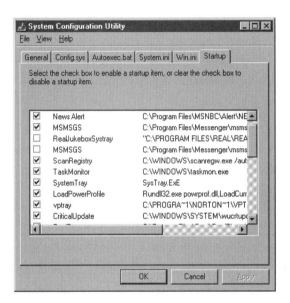

Explanation

Also, see if you can find out the make and model of your video card. This information may be in the documentation that came with your PC, or it may be listed by name in Display Adapters under the System icon in Control Panel. You can use technical Web sites like DriversHQ™ at www.drivershq.com and WinFiles at www.winfiles.com to look up your video card manufacturer by name and try to find more recent drivers (the software that configures your hardware to work under your operating system) for your video card. Then install them per the instructions on the download site.

Finally, it's possible that your WebSite Complete installation may somehow have become corrupted (perhaps during a crash or lockup on your PC). Use the instructions at the end of this appendix for uninstalling WebSite Complete, and then reinstall it using the instructions in Chapter 2.

Question

How can I recover pages I deleted from my Web project?

Answer

Unless you have a backup of your WebSite Complete Web project that contains these pages as they existed before you deleted them, you can't. This is also true if you delete a whole Web project. However, if you have a backup with the pages, go to the Restore option on the File menu and choose the Web project you want to restore.

Question

When I try to log in to Online Manager, I get an "access denied" message even though I'm providing the correct username and password.

Answer

Post a message on the Go Daddy message board at www.supportwebsite.com. Your account may not be properly set up; therefore you wouldn't have access to the management tool.

Question

I've built my site and its online store using WebSite Complete, but now I'd like to take a design I created in a different program and use it with WebSite Complete. Can I do that?

Answer

No. You can't use a Web design built outside of WebSite Complete with this software.

Question

Before I got this book, I found and installed an earlier version of WebSite Complete, which I'm still using. But I don't seem to have all of the features mentioned in this book. Plus my software keeps locking up, and I sometimes crash while working on my Web site. Will installing this most recent version solve my problems?

Answer

Yes. The version included with this book should help reduce or eliminate the lockups you're having. After the upgrade, you should see all the features discussed in this book.

Question

I previously had my own personal Web site and used FTP to upload my files. I still use FTP software. Can I use it to publish new pages and changes to my WebSite Complete–created site?

Answer

No. Doing so may cause problems with the storage of your site and how it displays and works for visitors. Use only WebSite Complete to publish your WebSite Complete–created project.

Working from More Than One PC with WebSite Complete

Since you can make changes to your Web site from any PC where you have an Internet connection and WebSite Complete installed, you may want to be able to publish changes from a second PC, which can be either your work or home PC, at your pleasure.

If the second PC doesn't already have WebSite Complete installed, run the setup from the CD, as you did in Chapter 2 for the first PC.

You also need to copy your Web project from the first PC to the second. Web projects you create in WebSite Complete are stored in a folder named for your project beneath the WebSite Complete folder at `C:\Program Files\WebSite Complete\`*yourprojectname*.

You can use Windows Explorer to copy the contents of your Web project along with the file named *yourdomainname*`.wcd` to a blank, formatted disk. Then take the disk to the other PC and use Windows Explorer again to create a folder beneath your WebSite Complete folder named identically as the project folder that appeared on your other PC. (For example, one of mine is `C:\Program Files\WebSite Complete\onespecialclick`.) Then copy your Web project from the disk to the new folder you just created.

Tip

If you use e-mail at both PCs, you can also mail yourself a copy of the files that go in your Web project folder.

Uninstalling WebSite Complete

You may at some point want to uninstall WebSite Complete—either because you want to reinstall it fresh or because you no longer want it installed on your system.

Here are the steps necessary to properly uninstall WebSite Complete:

1. With WebSite Complete closed, click Windows Start ➢ Settings ➢ Control Panel.

2. Double-click the Add/Remove Programs icon.

3. Locate and select WebSite Complete Deluxe Edition in the program list, and click Add/Remove.

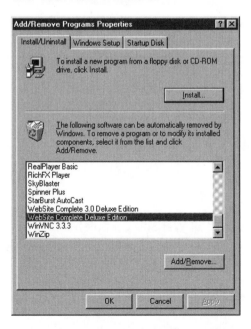

4. When prompted, choose Automatic Uninstall.

Be patient, because many files have to be removed. Once uninstalling is complete, you'll receive a confirmation window.

Glossary

ad views

refers to the number of times an ad is displayed on sites within that advertising network; ads usually change each time a Web visitor reloads or revisits a Web site with such advertising

bandwidth

overall connection capability

banner network ads

also called banner ads, these ads usually appear at the top or bottom of a Web site's main page and, when clicked, link a user to the site of the company whose ad is running

broken link

a link on a Web site that, when clicked, fails to produce the desired results (the Web page it's meant to open does not load)

buttons

Web site visitors click these navigational tools to link to a new page or tool

content

the meat and potatoes of any Web site, including any text or images that have been created especially for the site, but not including the templates that were designed to lay out the pages

database

a collection of information (data) that is organized on various key fields (product or customer name, for example) so that the stored data can be quickly retrieved

digital camera

a type of camera that saves pictures to electronic media, such as a smart card (looks like a tiny disk), rather than to film that must be developed

domain name

the registered name of a Web site

domain registration

the act of registering a Web site name with an authorized registering agent

e-commerce

the practice of selling products and services directly from an online location, such as a Web site or an online service

Flash Animation

a hot graphics applet, owned by a company named Macromedia, that can add a splashy and sometimes dramatic look to Web sites by using eye-catching, fast-loading, moving Web page graphics as an entry screen or as a special in-page image

Flash Generator
a helpful wizard that helps you select, modify, and generate a Flash animation for your Web site

Flash Intros
full-screen moving graphics leading into your Web site's home page

hypertext link (hyperlink)
special text on a Web page that, when clicked upon, opens a related page on the same or different Web site

Java
the programming language of the Internet

map link
a special type of Web hyperlink that connects a reference on a text page, such as a real estate listing, to an online map of that area

merchant account
a special type of Web hosting account that establishes your business' credit-worthiness, and sets up a way for financial transactions to be performed on your site (such as the processing of credit card orders)

meta tags
the HTML equivalent of search words

mouseover
a special effect applied to a button (or other object) on a Web page that allows the object to change appearance when a (mouse) cursor passes over it or clicks it

name server
a computer that contains a list of domain names and their corresponding IP addresses (like 63.241.136.30); when you type a domain name into a Web browser and you try to connect to the site, it's the job of the name server to associate that domain name with its IP address to make sure the correct Web site opens in the Web browser

navigational buttons
buttons used on a Web site, with labels such as Back and Next, that, when clicked upon, help a visitor move through the various pages of the site (or a long list of products and services available, such as in an online catalog)

newsgroups
messaging areas devoted to particular topics

page caching
depending on how your browser has been configured for use, revisiting a site may cause the site to load from a copy stored on your hard drive from the last session, not from the Web server itself

plug-in

a tool that can be plugged into and used from a Web page

search words

words that help identify and categorize a Web site on Internet search engines

site statistics

information about a site (who visited, where they were from, what pages they looked at, etc.) that can help you identify the level of traffic to your site and offers some indication of who your audience may be

smart posting

a method in which you publish only the pages or files of your site that have been changed since you last published

spam

unsolicited e-mail advertising

templates

blank Web page forms in which you can add text and images based upon the layout provided

time-out

a specified time that the Web server waits to respond before it decides that the server isn't going to respond and it should stop trying

traffic

the amount of visitors accessing a particular Web site, often measured in unique users per day, per week, or per month (with a server or online service, it refers to the number of people accessing the system during any given time)

virus-scanning software

also called antivirus software; designed to check your system for the presence of potentially harmful computer viruses that can affect the way your programs and/or your hardware performs

Web host provider

an individual or company that provides space to host a Web site, making it available to the public via the Internet and a Web browser

Web publishing

the process by which the files you create as you make your Web site are transferred to a Web server, subsequently making your e-commerce site accessible to others

Web rings

groups of Web sites that are tied together by some common theme, message, or content (including e-commerce in general and various types of online sales specifically)

Web servers

computers running specialized software that handles the behind-the-scenes publishing of Web sites to the Internet and that processes requests from visitors

Windows swap file

part of the Windows operating system that uses some of your hard-disk space as a virtual work space in which applications and data can be moved on and off the Desktop rapidly

Index

Note to the Reader: Throughout this index **boldfaced** page numbers indicate primary discussions of a topic. *Italicized* page numbers indicate illustrations.

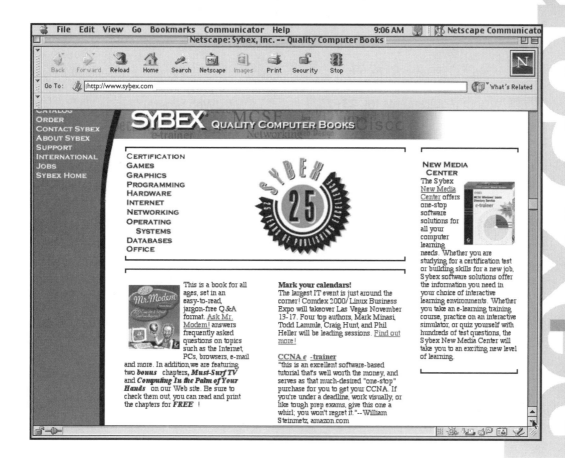

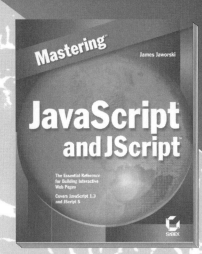
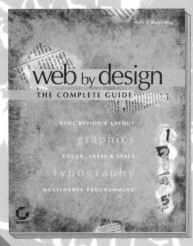

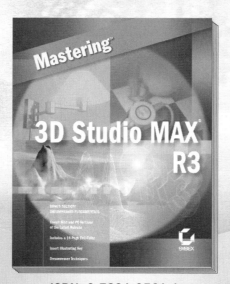

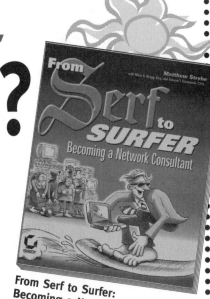

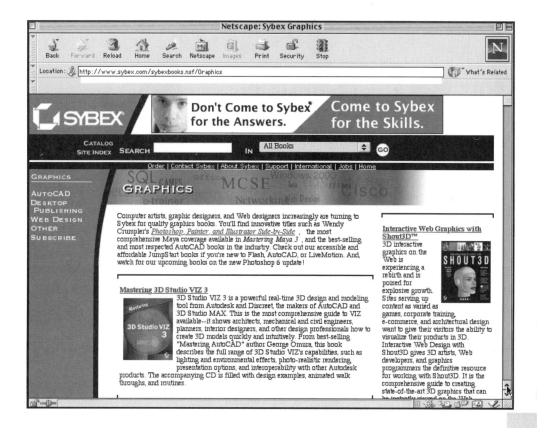

What Can You Do with
WebSite Complete 4.0?

Are you an entrepreneur looking to start an Internet business? A proprietor of a brick-and-mortar business you want to take online? A small business owner or independent contractor looking to advertise your services to a wider audience? With the software included in *Instant E-Commerce!*, setting up an e-commerce site is as easy as pointing, clicking, and imagining the possibilities.

Create an E-Commerce Site in No Time!

On the CD, you'll find a full version of Go Daddy Software's Website Complete 4.0—a $14.95 value *absolutely free*. With this do-it-yourself software, described in detail in the book, you'll be able to develop a fully functional e-commerce site without becoming a Web programmer—or paying for one. Better yet, when you're ready to launch your e-business, this CD is specially coded so that you get *$10 off* the $49.95 hosting fee for the first site you post with Go Daddy Software.

Use the treeview pane to add text, links, images, animations, and plug-ins.

Quickly add a specialized Web page to your site.

Build an online store.

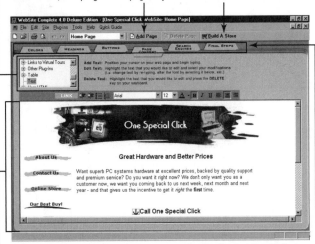

Place the cursor anywhere you want within the design window and start typing.

Use the Control Panel tabs to design and modify your site.

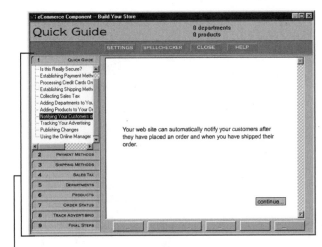

The E-Commerce Component Quick Guide steps you through each phase of the online store building process, from adding products to handling payment methods, shipping methods, and sales tax.

System Requirements

To use this software, you need to have the following:

- Windows 95/98/2000 or Windows NT 4.0 (Service Pack 3). WebSite Complete 4.0 does not operate on Apple Macintosh operating systems.
- Dial-up Internet connection with an Internet Service Provider.
- Microsoft Internet Explorer version 5.0 or greater. (Don't have it? It's on the CD.)
- RAM: Windows ME, 32MB; Windows 98, 16MB (32MB recommended); Windows 2000, 32MB; Windows NT 4.0, 32MB.

- Hard-drive free space: 17.2MB (additional space may be required for Internet Explorer 5.0).
- Color display: 16-bit or greater (recommended); 256-color supported.
- CD-ROM drive.
- Sound card (recommended).